Fiddling Through
The Wilderness

To the Mazzenga family —
When you turn Toward the
Lord, you enjoy the journey.
I did. — Blessings
Edna.

Fiddling Through The Wilderness

Edna Falciglia Panaggio

To order additional copies of this book, contact:
Xlibris Corporation
1-888-795-4274
www.Xlibris.com
Orders@Xlibris.com
77496

Contents

I dedicate this book
to all those mentioned,
who contributed to the
messages these
experiences provided,
beginning
in

Baltimore, Maryland,

the true meaning of love,
confession, trust, forgiveness,
faith, joy, rewards, and promises
the
mighty power of God, who
lives within us,
delivers in our hearts
from his Son, Jesus Christ
through our obedience
to His word.

And

my son, my daughter, and her
four beautiful children,
Jesse, Molly, Colin, and Caleb.

Preface

This book is the living truth on how God faithfully comes into one's life, if one allows Him to, and uses us to His glory.

After I had accepted Jesus into my life, I prayed for him to guide me always. I vowed to get to know him better by studying the Holy Bible and prayed also that I would be given the knowledge to understand what I must do to fulfill His will for my life. Once I began searching, I learned of the gifts that are in the Holy Spirit as described in Galatians 5:22—love, joy, peace, patience, goodness, kindness, faithfulness, gentleness, and self-control. I vowed to use these gifts as much as possible with all people who come into my life, whether of my religious faith or not. I am convinced that we are all God's people and together we can learn to serve Him faithfully.

My Holy Spirit urges me to follow this path and to spread God's word as much as I am able. It is in this way that I endeavor to serve God more fully. My heart is filled with great joy when I can connect to God through my prayers and can help others to do so as well.

Recently, I have learned to use the words *thank you* more often, especially in my prayers. I thank Him for urging me to write my experiences. I thank Him for connecting me with people whose grief, tears, anxiety, agony, and pain I can help to lessen through my introduction to His teaching and love. I thank Him for that.

I welcome all of you to join me in my quest and know you will find that He will be there waiting for you to experience the excitement He created for your life, as He did mine. Hopefully, this book will begin that journey for you.

Introduction

The year 1981 and the last twenty-nine and one-half years of marriage are about to be behind me. Those years between then and now have transformed me into someone that I could never have imagined.

The pastor of our Catholic church called me on the phone to ask me why I was attending the meetings of troubled singles within the church. After my explanation, I asked him to contact my husband for counseling. He did not. I met a woman, the mother of my daughter's friend, at choir rehearsal. I remember it so clearly. She had married a Catholic, raised her family Catholic, but was raised herself as a child and young adult in the Presbyterian faith. Noticing my weakness, she said to me one day, "You do not know the Lord as you should. Why don't you join me in Bible study through the Christian Women's Club?" She had started praying for her husband, who was a very rich, successful alcoholic neglecting the growth of their five children. Prayer had achieved healing him of his habit. My daughter and her daughter became close friends. They sought refuge from their alcoholic homes, exploring Charismatic meetings in another Catholic church. My pastor did not support those meetings. I took it upon myself to explore my daughter's venue where I found a peace beyond all understanding. My life began its change.

Liquor had taken its priority between my husband and myself. We had focused our life on partying, social clubs, and some pretty heavy drinking. It all started during his college days. We brought a son and daughter into the world. Alcohol contributed to many challenges in the growth of our children's lives.

I stayed in Maryland during our separation and ultimate divorce when I refused to drink with him any longer. I continued to praise and worship Jesus as my savior. My son and daughter, during this period of time being old enough to move out, really never pursued any college education. Their efforts and good habits eventually started to take hold to shape their lives as I continued to pray for them. They both eventually moved to Rhode Island and started on their individual paths.

Old Lives Were Drawing To A Close

One would think that my life was drawing to a close, but I was being born again.

After twenty-five years of living in Maryland, looking back, I saw vivid pictures of that life's new beginning of August 1963.

We had arrived as a married couple with a boy, nine, and a girl, five, to begin a new life. We moved to Maryland since American Totalizator bought out Grant Money Meters, the company my husband was employed by. The larger company had asked him to come along with the purchase. Moving from north to south would be quite an adjustment for all of us. There were great promises and uncertainty of what this transfer would turn out to be. While my husband had left before we did, upon joining him, he had found a house to rent in a neighborhood just changing from white to black. On the first day of moving in, my nine-year-old son came home, bleeding from the forehead while trying to find new friends to play with. We were surrounded by white families, mostly Catholic, and after treating the injury and my young son's feeling of rejection, I approached the parent next door where the mishap had taken place. This mother immediately came out of her house, fearful that I would enter, to extend her arm and demand I leave her yard. "We do not want black people in my yard," said she in front of my children. Granted, I was pretty dark, and so were my son and daughter. We had spent a month on the beach in Rhode Island before moving down south while my husband had started working and was looking for a place to live. This had seemed to him a fairly nice neighborhood, well kept, renting from an Italian man who was quite colorful and nice with a good family, who kept his property in good repair. They had shared a time of getting to know each other around a table of wine, cheese, and Italian bread—a showing of warmth that would have appealed to a family of our standing.

We enrolled the children in Catholic education, my son in a private Catholic military school since he was repeating the third grade and my daughter in the Catholic school nearby. David had to travel, taking two buses. We thought that would be quite traumatic for him, but having two cars and meeting an eighth grader that bussed to the same school who was happy to big-brother our son, the transportation problem would be solved. Our second car was pretty old with grunts and groans, but it worked. It was a prestigious school with lots of very new and shiny cars pulling up one by one. My son lived through a lot of embarrassment when I would go to pick him up in my old car, and he asked me to please not pick him up from school. We were a struggling family—new job, new rental, son with asthma and a learning disability due to premature birth. We chose the school because it was private. When we arrived in Maryland, since he was repeating a grade, we had him psychologically tested. The school was recommended to us. The military garb was extremely expensive. The discipline was rigid. It was hard for a young child who was already having emotional problems. He took up drum playing and was able to play in the band until he was criticized for his unusual marching due to a motor problem. It seemed that one of the teachers made disparaging remarks to this young child moving south from the north where he never learned to use the words *sir* and *ma'am*.

Our daughter did well under the "cane," in her Catholic school, from a nun who would lift it and loudly hit it to the floor in the first-year classroom. It was their way of using scare tactics that my children never contended with in Rhode Island. I soon found a job, saved some money, and after three years, was able to purchase a home farther north in Lutherville, Maryland. The children began public school. Our Catholic upbringing with the children switched to just Sundays. Dad changed jobs as assistant director of a state agency, and through the following years, our social lives were soaring. We found friends, Italian organizations, different groups and were partying with lots of drinking.

We were changing. Alcohol became a large part of our life. It was dangerous. My husband was traveling on his new job. I was working,

holding the fort with the children and working on their m⌐
much needed. We were spending a lot and not saving for ⌐
education.

My son began to show emotional signs of despair and was hospitaliz⌐
at age fifteen, which led to a change in his life. It was good, and we
are thankful that God had that plan for him. My husband and I needed
counseling. There were advantages to what we all learned that carried on
to make changes in his life. He left school in the eighth grade, worked
at odd jobs, received his high school equivalency at age seventeen left
home as a drummer, and never returned to live with us again. He is a
very good son and is a considerate, loving husband to a very wonderful
woman—a graduate nurse he met in Iowa after a divorce from his first
wife. His first wife always remained a good friend to him until her death.
I might add here that I prayed on my hands and knees when he left for
Iowa to study in a school, learning to repair wind instruments. I prayed
he'd find his way, and please, Lord, let him find a nurse as his next mate.
The Lord heard my prayer.

Our daughter, at age seventeen, after graduation from high school,
began to seek the Lord. She spent some time with the Lamb of God
Community, the group she met through St. Joseph's Catholic Church's
Charismatic group in Texas, Maryland. After leaving them six weeks later,
she attended college in Southern Maryland for one semester; but when a
very dear young male friend of hers committed suicide, she left, never to
return again. Later she attended community college where she majored
in dance. She studied to be an aesthetician, and later, after our divorce,
she moved to Rhode Island to live with a cousin. She became the first
aesthetician in Rhode Island to work with a salon owner. She later met
her husband to be at the Trinity Assembly of God. By that time, I also
was attending the Trinity Assembly of God in Maryland.

All this had been a blessing. God kept the love of this family together
as we all began to walk the walk individually—father, mother, son, and
daughter—each entering our own wilderness.

Female Priesthood

Jack

I was flying home from Bermuda. My loving friendship was over. I had made peace with the Lord and vowed I would take the trip to sever my relationship with Gus. It was a very difficult decision for me since he had been the person that had filled the void in my life. I had never met a man who was so concerned and loving. Our personalities were so similar. He was not the tall, dark, handsome man I had always dreamed of. On the contrary, he was just my height, well built and muscular, very athletic since he sailed, played golf very well, and was a competitive tennis player. He was somewhat bald and was crippled with arthritis.

On his first trip to the States, he was being evaluated for his arthritis at Baltimore's world-known hospital by a famous physician. I was working as a secretary and office manager for a physician who was very proficient in hair transplants. Gus, on his trip, had heard of this physician and came into the office to explore his candidacy for transplant. The doctor gave him a positive evaluation, and Gus made an appointment to get the work done while he was in the States. We kept in touch and became longtime foreign friends. We had both experienced marriage and divorce and decided never to marry again.

I learned much of his background and found he was one of twelve children. He and his family migrated from the Azores, Portugal, lived in England where his father was pastor of a nondenominational church, and finally settled in Bermuda after his divorce. His knowledge of the Bible was very helpful to me in my progress. We spent much of our time together conversing and enjoying my new adventure in things of the Spirit. He led me to the fact that I should only be affiliated with churches based on Jesus. He was kind and caring and loved by all who met him.

Upon my return, I knew of my transformation. I had committed my life to servanthood with the Lord. On the trip home, I was seated next to a woman like myself who shared her stories since her rebirth. We were kindred spirits with similar experiences.

During my time in Bermuda, Jack, the father of one of my dearest friends, Eudice, had been sent to a hospital and was in grave condition. He was elderly and had suffered from pneumonia before I left for Bermuda. Early morning after my return, I called Eudice, inquiring about her dad's grave condition. I was saddened to hear he was comatose. Eudice was glad to hear from me since just before he went into coma, he had called for me. It would be a matter of hours. Eudice insisted that I make every effort to visit him before his death. Of course, I agreed; and in my haste and confusion as to what the Lord had in store for me, I immediately called Sid Roth, the Jewish Christian pastor/radio host who was about to go on the air that morning at nine. It was eight thirty, and he was there at the studio answering the phone. I explained the situation that I was a newborn Christian and needed his guidance and assistance in praying with a Jewish man who was dying. I learned that after being born again, one naturally became involved in evangelism. That freedom calls a love to share with others. He advised me to bring my Bible with me. He advised me to pray without ceasing, and the Lord would speak through me. "*Speak through me*? What do you mean?" "Just that, just stay in prayer and try to read to him from the book of Isaiah," said he.

I showered, dressed, and got ready to leave for my appointed mission for the day. Oh, I was getting a big charge from all this. The excitement of being a messenger for the Lord turned out to be quite a role for this stage actress of forty years. I dramatically wrapped my Bible in a brown paper bag to fit, looked ready for the challenge, got into the driver's seat of my Toyota Corolla, and talked to the Lord all the way down to the front door of this Jewish hospital. My meeting with Eudice was scheduled for noon. Jack, her dad, would remind anyone who knew him of George Burns, husband of Gracie Allen, a husband-and-wife comedy team known from radio and TV. Jack was a real character that I grew to love since he was a dear friend of my ex-husband, who had hired him to work as an administrative assistant at the age of seventy-five for the Department of Social Services as a senior employee. Jack became a father to Pat, took him under his wing, and taught him to smoke cigars and play the horses. A really lovable character. Jack was devastated when Pat and I separated. He loved us both as his children. As a matter of fact, since I was well into acting and modeling, I had a photographer take head shots of Jack just two months before he became ill and registered him with an agent to try his skills at making commercials. In a full-body shot of Jack, the photographer characterized him in a soft hat, dress suit, and holding his cigar. A pose that George Burns used in *his* publicity shots. Unfortunately, he never even got to audition. I do remember, however, that his granddaughter, who married after his death, had this same picture at her wedding reception. Her grandfather was not to miss her wedding.

I took the elevator to the third floor. Eudice met me at the elevator and welcomed me with open arms and a deep hug. We both became teary eyed at the happiness of being together at this very important time in both our lives. I asked if I could read from the Bible to her father. "No," said Eudice, "we don't know the Lord like you do, and it would upset my family, I am sure." I understood. I knew now that the Holy Spirit was in charge. After some time together, I was not coherent to answer any of the questions regarding my trip to Bermuda that Eudice was trying to discuss. My mind and heart were focused on what and where I was going on *this* trip.

After about one-half hour of visiting with the family, Eudice left the group and headed for the room where her father lay in a coma. She went before me to pave the way. While she was with him, I stayed at the opening of the room and began to recite the words I learned in my Catholic upbringing, the Lord's Prayer. I silently started and continued, "Our Father, who art in heaven," and so forth. At the end of the prayer, a dramatic thing happened. Jack began to convulse. Eudice started yelling, "I have never seen him do this before!" She ran out of the room, calling for the doctor. During all this drama, the family was completely oblivious to what was going on. I gracefully went to the side of the bed. As soon as I approached the bed, Jack calmed down. I leaned over and close to his ear. I told him that he could call upon God, ask forgiveness of his sins, accept that forgiveness, and believe. God had already intervened. It was so easy. It was brief, I thought, but then there wasn't much time. The doctor would soon arrive. God knew the whole picture anyway, from beginning to end. I had done my part and left the rest to Him. At that point, Jack came up from his pillow, looked straight at me, waved his right hand to the heavens, and calmly placed his head back on the pillow.

Eudice came running in with the female doctor that was in attendance, and I went back to the entrance of the room where I was when Eudice ran out of the room. As the doctor left, she said, thinking I was one of the family, "He'll be all right now. He has calmed down." I said, "Yes, I know." My mission was accomplished. At four o'clock the next morning, Jack was gone.

I didn't want the family to know of my performance that day. I asked the Lord to simply pass the word on to them, at His timing. It was more than six months later, at one of our frequent dinners with Jacks's wife, Belle, and Eudice at Jack's home when I told the story. Belle had been questioning life after death. I explained what had happened at the hospital as I prayed with Jack, and she understood completely. She believed that the Lord was within us and Jack was with God. Eudice, on the other hand, bellowed out at me, telling me she never wanted to see me again. Time went on without any communication from Eudice for almost a year. Palm Sunday of the following year, Eudice called me. I never ceased praying for her and Belle and their family. They were family to me. (One time, during my marriage, she had me stay with her for a week when her husband and son had gone on vacation. She knew the distress I was living with in my home.) Eudice said she could no longer live without her best friend. She had been terribly disturbed for all this time without my friendship. We stayed really close for many years to follow, and Eudice called me frequently with spiritual concerns and questions about the Lord and God. Belle died a few years after Jack. I had moved back to Rhode Island, where I would live until this day. When I would visit Belle and Eudice, I slept in Jack's twin bed in Belle's apartment; and through the night, we would talk about the things of God and heaven. Eudice passed away in the year 2006. During her illness, she would call me with many questions about after death. I loved Eudice. She had chutzpah and exercised it with seminars. I know through prayer that Eudice met her demise in complete peace.

Over a month ago, I received a call from their daughter who lives in Chicago. She was in Baltimore because her father has passed on. Her brother, in his early fifties, lived in Baltimore in subsidized living with a type of mental retardation. His mother had arranged those living conditions when he was old enough to live on his own. He was quite independent with good health care. I, of course, was concerned since her brother had been caregiving, in a sense, to his dad. I knew that Eudice would have been very concerned because at one time she asked me if I would look after her son should she go before him. She always said that she wanted to take him with her. Three weeks after Bernie's death, I had a call from a dear friend of theirs in Baltimore, who said that the son died after his dad was buried. Ironic.

Phil

After my divorce, I attended a nondenominational Christian church. I joined their sixty-person choir and grew to love the church and its educational process. On Sunday mornings after service, a group of friends would spend most of the day together with some of the elders of the church. We would have brunch together, usually at my apartment, spend the day with the Lord, and get ready for the evening service again. I actually took baptism, being fully dipped in a pool of water at the age of fifty-five, and came up dedicating my life in service to the Holy Spirit.

My dear friend Eudice was concerned that I would be alone, and she was standing by, waiting for me to accept dating again. One day, she called to tell me of a wonderful Italian lawyer that her nephew was working for, whose son had committed suicide, and in their distressful life, the wife one day cleaned out the house of all the furniture and everything they owned together and left him high and dry. When he arrived home that evening, he was absolutely traumatized.

My concern for his welfare and comfort was important to me. I therefore agreed to meet him. When Phil called me, we made arrangements to meet after my choir rehearsal on Thursday evening. He could sit through the rehearsal, and afterward we planned to stop for coffee. He agreed that would be fine.

Thursday night, Phil was not in the church. He was outside waiting for me in his car. When I approached him, he said, "I have never seen such beautiful smiling faces coming out of a church before. What do you do in there?" I asked him why he did not come in, and he said he did not feel worthy to enter a church because of his past life. I followed him in my own car, and we stopped for coffee and dessert in a lovely, cozy coffee shop with delicate Italian pastries. He poured his heart out to me, and I learned a lot about him. He never stopped talking. He was large in stature, loved to eat, ate compulsively, and gave me a very vivid picture of his past.

He had lived a very easy life in an Italian household. His father doted upon him and always made sure he had money in his pocket. He always had his own way. He had a sister whom he had not seen in years, actually, since his mother had passed on. She lived close by, but they had been estranged due to his lifestyle. His mother died soon after his father. She had refused to see Phil before her death.

He and his wife never had natural children but adopted a boy. The boy grew up in Catholic schools, had been in counseling for some time, evidently was a very distressed child, and at the age of seventeen, committed suicide.

At this point, I had hoped I didn't bite off more than I could chew. I didn't want to step before the Lord. I proceeded with great caution and was careful not to become too close. I felt his pain. In his way of being kind, he would fill my freezer with meats from his special Italian stores in Little Italy, fill my refrigerator with fruits and vegetables, and wanted to take me out to restaurants to eat meals. I was smothered and boldly had to stop all that. I became very disturbed by this behavior. He did, however, begin to attend church with me and fellowship with my Christian friends.

Soon after we met, he asked me to go with him to see his sister. He called her and made arrangements. I, of course, was happy to be part of that meeting and prayed that it would be a happy reunion. I met a lovely woman with her husband who welcomed her brother into her home. We dined, and as we parted, we all embraced. And there was forgiveness for their past behavior toward each other. His sister showed great appreciation to me. I really didn't do anything but was just obedient to the Spirit within me, whose plan we fulfilled. I was grateful for this wonderful occasion.

Another day, after a service, he asked me to accompany him at the grave of his son. He had purchased one dozen red roses to put into two vases that were situated outside of the crypt. It was twenty-one degrees, a bitter, cold winter day. The ice that had formed on the bottom of the vases needed to be chipped away to make room for the roses. He gave me six roses, and he and I put the roses into each vase. Suddenly, right before our eyes, all twelve roses started to open up. I couldn't believe what I was seeing, and neither did he. I remember he said, "What is happening here? What do you think this means? Do you think my son is in heaven? What is going on?" I was as bewildered as he, but God consoled him by speaking through me and saying, "I think your son is saying, 'It's okay dad, I am at peace.'"

It was soon after that Phil began to show some behavior that was very strange. I began to see what was hidden in his heart that was crippling him. He was using money freely, and I couldn't understand or know for sure where the money was coming from. It was publicized finally that he, as president of a savings and loan company, had access to an account belonging to his ex-wife, who engaged her own lawyer and went to the press to expose him. He freely was using money of some of his clients to put another client into a barroom business. With full exposure and publicity, he was found guilty and was stripped of his law practice.

He suffered heavy depression. He stopped by my apartment one day and had returned, in a big black plastic bag you would throw trash into, a Bible I had bought for him, along with other things that he did not want. They were left at the door of my apartment, which I found as I was leaving for work one morning. I had not heard from him for a long time but continued to pray for him. I tried to find out where he was, but no one seemed to know. I remembered that one day a while back, he said, "I wish I could find a quiet island where I could be away from everything I have done and the people I have hurt." Soon, I heard he had stripped his apartment of the things he had, locked himself in, and was eventually carried out and put into an institution where he finally died. He had found his island.

John

As an actress, I was dabbling in producing and directing. I was asked to direct *The Man Who Came to Dinner* at a community theater. John auditioned for the lead role. John showed a great deal of talent as an actor and was new to the community. I became very interested in his background as we became friends. He was in his late twenties but rather mature. He had just come out of the seminary, studying to be a priest. He was living in the priest's house of my parish. The assistant pastor took him in with hope of helping him through a nervous breakdown after leaving the seminary. I never questioned him about that. My nature is not to question anyone for what or where or who they are. It really doesn't matter. The Lord will show me what I must do to comfort his children's hearts. He was a talented actor, and he gave the role everything it needed. He seemed very happy working with the cast and made many friends.

John began to heal through his friends and newfound hobby. He gradually left the church house and started nursing school.

It was about five years since we'd seen each other. We were both very busy with our lives, working in different directions. I had my family commitments, work, and my hobby with the theater. Our paths had not met in all that time.

Soon, I received a call from a dear friend of mine, who would be playing Yente in *Fiddler on the Roof* at the summer theater of Towson University. She had originally been asked to do the role of Golde but was found to be too tall for the chosen Tevye. She had played Golde with another company when I played Yente, and we had remained good friends. The chosen Tevye would be John. I was pleased to be chosen to play the role of Golde with John. The director was happy with the selection.

The play went off without a hitch. We rehearsed many nights a week up to the time of production. It was hard for me as wife and mother, but the acting bug had me a long time before I was married for sure. We were a match even though we had such an age difference. It really didn't matter at all. During rehearsals, however, John was showing signs of illness. Always tired. He was gray. The cast became very aware, but they were all tired holding down jobs or being students, and no one really thought it was serious. The play went on to great reviews.

John disappeared again from my life. I always thought of him and prayed for him. My instincts were that he was not well but didn't know how to contact him.

About four months later, Paula, one of the musical directors from the Jewish Community Center who had been in touch with John, called me. "Did you know about John? He has AIDS. He is in the hospital in the last stages. I thought you would want to know." All I could say was "Do you think he would like me to pray with him?" Without hesitation, she said yes.

I responded immediately. I called the hospital. I found that he was in a private room and was able to receive guests between the hours of two and four. I began to get ready to drive down to the hospital. I prayed before I went. My prayer was that he would be alone, with no one to interfere with our meeting. I brought the Bible Phil had brought back to me and planned to read of the goodness of God. I was aware of the end that AIDS patients had to face in their final days.

I arrived at the hospital at 2:30 p.m. I was greeted by a very frail-looking young man that had been informed by the attending nurse that I would be visiting John. He was John's friend. The nurse had given both of them the message. John was in the bathroom and would be out momentarily. The friend disappeared. When John came out of the bathroom, we hugged each other, and the first words that came out of John's mouth were "I'm afraid to die." I understood. I listened to his every word as he confessed and seemed to repent. He cried as he spoke, and my throat filled up with good cause. As a seminary student, I assumed John probably knew the Lord better than I and should have faith in knowing that He was a loving God and understood everything. I read certain scriptures from the Bible that I had ready to support him in his belief. I took all the time needed to comfort him in his fright, and when I left, he showed less anxiety than when I arrived. No one ever interfered with our conversation, which was answer to my prayer.

When I left, I knew I would never see John again. It wasn't long after that he returned to his home, back with his parents, and died there.

John was good at what he did. He was a good friend to everyone he met. He was very effective as a caring nurse to his patients. He enjoyed doing many interesting roles through the theater, whose friends thought a lot of him and loved him. He used his gifts well.

Matthew 6:19-21, NIV, says, "Don't store up for yourselves treasures on earth, where moth and rust destroy, and where thieves break in and steal. But store up for yourselves treasures in heaven, where moth and rust do not destroy, and where thieves do not break in and steal. For where your treasure is, there your heart will be also" (see epilogue Fiddler on the Roof).

Baltimore Diaries

Sandy

During the interim of my separation and divorce, I joined the Marriott Hotel swim club where one day, in my attempt to relax from my stressful life, I had an asthma attack in the pool. I got out of the pool immediately, waved everyone away from me until it subsided, and finally ended up sitting next to a woman who had watched the process. I met my first Christian Jew, who began to tell me of a swallowing problem she'd had for years. We began talking of being born again. She was a member of the Assembly of God Church in Lutherville, not far from where I lived. Sandy invited me to go with her one Sunday. She knew I would love the music since during our friendly conversation, she learned of my musical involvement. It was the beginning. I became a regular at that church, joined the choir and the singles group, attended their Bible studies, and Sandy and I became lifelong friends. We saw eye to eye on many things.

* * *

Trisha

My path through the wilderness was widening. The adopted daughter of our married friends dropped into my life as I attended the Assembly of God. She had married and had two children. She and her husband divorced because both were on drugs, and at this time, she and her nine-year-old daughter were living with a much older man and his teenage daughter.

He wasn't very stable without a permanent job, and Patricia was ready to get out of the relationship. She had a son living with her mother and dad, but that situation wasn't very healthy. Her father was a heavy drinker. She confided that she was being introduced to the Lord by a working friend who was interested in her situation and invited her to a born-again church. In a weak moment, I invited her to come to live with me. Since I only had one bedroom, I checked with the apartment manager and found that there was a larger apartment with two and a half bedrooms available in the complex. The rent would be larger, but Trisha had a good job and could help with the increase. Before she moved in, I heard at one of our services that it would be advisable to get rid of all sins while working with the Holy Spirit. The pastor specifically mentioned hard rock music. It would be mandatory in order to put the Holy Spirit to work within us. In my obedience, I made sure she got rid of a collection of hard rock records, about a $2,000 collection, before she moved in with me. I was much further along in my walk, and I wasn't taking any chances. She was not a happy camper about the idea, but I, in no way, would have them brought into my apartment. We took them out of the trunk of her car outside of the building and literally broke each one on our knees and threw all fragments into the trash bin. It worked. I would also invite her husband to frequent visits for dinner to be with the children.

One night we had an experience with bad things going on in the apartment building. Her son was involved. The police showed up. There seemed to be an evil spell in the building. At Bible study, we brought the gathering together in agreement against what was happening. That evening, a howling dog was outside the building, and I thought I was the only one that heard it. It started at 3:00 a.m. and continued on until 6:00 a.m. Patricia got up at that point, and in one of her moods, she was ranting about this dog outside that was wailing all night. She wanted to let the dog in to feed him. He was right outside our sliding door, scratching at the screen. We lived on the first floor. I insisted that she ignore it and pray it away. I had been praying for those three hours, on my knees, waving any illness from the spirits to leave the building. In my positive trust in the promises of the Lord, this dog was confirmation as answer to our prayer at Bible study. I brought her attention to Mark 5:11-14: "A large herd of pigs was feeding on a hill near there. The demons begged Jesus, 'Send us into the pigs; let us go into them.' So Jesus allowed them to do this. Then the herd of pigs—about two thousand of them—rushed down the hill into the lake and were drowned." Trish understood and closed the blinds on the sliding door, and eventually the dog left, never to be seen again. Nor had we ever seen him in the neighborhood before that night. He was an ugly-shaped white dog with pink eyes. The next day, the family that was involved in the event moved out, and all was peaceful within the building after that. Obedience wins again.

Trisha finally reunited and remarried her ex-husband and had a third child. I filled the void in my apartment with another young woman who was in dire need. That was Cindy. She moved in, attended Bible studies, accepted the Lord to be her savior, and eventually followed me to Rhode Island.

*   *   *

Andy

The Lord sent me Trish's brother, whom I also knew. His mother called me and asked for my help. He was an alcoholic, stealing out of liquor stores and taking drugs with a bunch of so-called friends who supported his habit. One day, in my search for him, I found him with a girl who begged me to help him. He was probably eighteen years of age. I contacted his doctor, and he admitted him into the hospital. We worked together so that he would not discharge him until I find a Christian facility. I found Teen Challenge. The only opening they had was in Virginia. After I had made full arrangements for him to be admitted, I drove him there. On the ride down, I told him the training and learning he would receive there would be his salvation. He had to leave after a week because they were not in a position to administer the medication prescribed to him. The Lord had already started to work in him. When he left, he was no longer drinking or taking drugs and married the girlfriend that was pregnant without being sure this child was his; and when I last spoke with his family, he was well on his way to being a good father and provider for this woman he married on faith. Last I heard, he had five children.

*   *   *

Lights, Camera, Action

I was continuing on my acting career. I had finally signed with two agencies, which kept me pretty busy as a professional model/actress being cast in industrials, commercials, fashion shows while I continued with my freelance productions with my solely owned company, E&P Productions, Inc., running musicals for an exclusive dinner club and surrounding country clubs, which helped to support me financially. I also worked for a law firm part-time. I pounded the pavements for acting work when I met Robin, who was with a casting company. She cast me in my first commercial. Robin and I became friends. She was Jewish, had a very little child, and was separated from her husband. She started attending my Bible studies, where she accepted Jesus as her Messiah. She eventually married an enterprising Jewish Christian who blends well with her, and they have both taken *alyah* (citizenship) in Israel.

I felt the Lord leading me in all different directions, taking care not to allow me to be too free with my freedom. I was very open to Him. I accepted to be baptized in this church. I actually was dunked into the pool and came up dedicating my life to God from that day forward.

My acting career soared when I walked into an advertising agency and was cast in a radio commercial with three other top radio actors as a spokesperson for a man running for senator of Wisconsin. One of my model agencies cast me for a U.S. government industrial film, and because of these two jobs back-to-back, I was able to join Screen Actors Guild (SAG) and the American Federation of Television and Radio Artists (AFTRA) unions. I was well on my way.

I became involved in community acting for colleges and organizations, which enriched my talent and brought me into producing and directing. Since my husband and I were members of a private dinner club, the Greenspring Inn, I interviewed with the owner and planned an audition with top semiprofessionals like myself, the top stage talent of Baltimore, as I incorporated E&P Productions. All this was in the 1980s. Those were good and happy days that took me through my separation, divorce, and healing.

The word traveled fast that I had a very unique company, and the jobs rolled in for other elite organizations and clubs. We did a showboat performance featuring Buddy Wachter, onetime child protégé of Fred Waring, who played a banjo like no one I ever heard before. One banjo with ten fingers, sounding like three banjos. Ironically, the management had a showboat set in the archives of the club. I discovered a young nine-year-old Annie that someone requested we feature in one of my musicals. Another talent I found on the cover of *Baltimore* magazine as "People to Watch in 1982" was Joey, a new talent find, fifteen-year-old sensational dancer/singer. We featured him in another one of our productions.

Falls and Valley Roads
Lutherville, Maryland 21093
823-8600

January 20, 1981

Dear Member,

SHOW TIME RETURNS - The acceptance of our dinner Show in the Fall was excellent. We are pleased to be able to bring you a New Musical Comedy Review of songs by Charles Strouse, composer of Broadway Musicals such as Annie, Bye-Bye Birdie, Applause and others. This delightful, humorous, musical review will reaquaint you with familiar songs and introduce you to other songs you'll become friends with right away. Presented by E & P Productions, the show is choreographed to give more than just wonderful songs. The show stopper of the night should be our 11 year old red head singing songs from "Annie".

I was led to the previous year's Miss Maryland, who had won with opera talent. We produced a performance of Italian arias with male support from the Peabody Institute. We sold the entertainment to a Jewish country club, which featured a complete Italian buffet. This spectacular ended with "Way Compare" (the song about musical instruments), inviting the audience to join in by following a parade on the dance floor, pretending to play instruments to close the performance. It brought the house down. We brought joy wherever we went.

We brought a group from our church to the Inn at Christmas and finished two great performances of the musical *Come Celebrate Jesus* when management, after the first performance, suggested our second performance we use less Jesus. Out of our ten performers, three bowed out. They felt that in their obedience, they needed to follow the Lord. I pursued as director and simply sat back and watched the cast divide. On the second performance, we had less singers, but God's angels joined the choir. There were definitely more voices than the day before. My obedience in continuing in the request of management made a child aged five leave her parent's table and take over the whole dance floor alone, dancing to the song we sang in the score for children. She was dressed in a perky white organdy dress, wearing a white headpiece on her blond hair. Needless to say, she was the littlest angel. It was a miracle. The obedient few that stayed with me joined me in praise. God had His way in our service.

E&P entertained for the Shriners to a full hall of people and brought the house down as they responded with stomping feet, yelling, "More, more, more."

Someone called me one evening to bring my attention to an article in the newspaper that reported that our "group was in real demand." Nostalgia was very big, and on behalf of Baltimore talent, Edna was recognized by Mayor Schaefer, who named her to "Baltimore's Best List." All this in God's plan, I thought.

What did I do to deserve all this?

At Cross Keys Inn

Nostalgia Makes A Comeback

By Zelma Holzgang

Edna Panaggio's spare-time hobby is fast becoming a full-time business.

About a year and a half ago, Mrs. Panaggio visited the Green Spring Inn on Falls Road and decided, despite the pleasant ambience of the place, that it lacked a certain something.

"Maybe a kind of mini-concert of show songs," she suggested to Green Spring's Toni Petty.

Mr. Petty decided to give it a try. He booked a show Ms. Panaggio worked up, featuring a handful of seasoned local performers, for a slow Tuesday night. The customers were so enthusiastic about the show, *Broadway in Concert*, the show ran for four more nights. E & P Productions was born.

Now Ms. Panaggio, the company's producer and director, is caught up in rehearsals for a nostalgic musical review, *It's Entertainment*, scheduled for Sunday evenings, March 14 and 21, at Cross Keys Inn. The show follows on the heels of two other E & P nostalgic successes, *Music America* and *Love Is Music*, "all choreographed and put together with comedy, glamour, and lots of happiness," as Mrs. Panaggio likes to say.

Her company has just completed a five-week run at Green Spring Inn, and has also

vaudevillian on the renowned Keith Circuit, and her mother, a pianist.

"As children, we were always encouraged to put on shows," she recalls. "When I was in grade school, I played *Heidi* on a local radio station, and I've been in and around show business ever since."

Moving to Baltimore 19 years ago, she began to search out little theater groups within the community.

"I've appeared with The Spotlighters, Baltimore Actors Theater, Essex Community College's Cockpit in the Court, as well as the Vagabond Players' production of *The Drunkard*.

Edna Panaggio

Christin Panaggio, Dennis Knight, Edna Panaggio and Bill Bevans: "Suddenly we're in real demand.

Memory Lane

By Zelma M. Holzgang

She's a Gemini. That means she's both future-oriented and nostalgic.

Which just happens to be a perfect description of Timonium's Edna Panaggio, presently knee-deep in rehearsals for the latest presentation of her memory-filled musical review, *It's Entertainment*.

"Each time I do one of these nostalgia pieces, I get as caught up

*   *   *

Suddenly, the Spirit Was Grieving

An experience I shall never forget, however, was an evening that I felt a deep depression and that I was being attacked by recollections of some of my past actions. I felt I needed someone to pray over me. I knew this wasn't from God, so I called a close Christian friend who would take me to a prayer meeting that she knew of. It was in a nonsectarian church that had weekly prayer meetings for people like me. I was really down on myself. Seven or eight people gathered in the form of a circle when in deep prayer with the pastor leading, he said, "Someone here is battling with their spirit." I immediately claimed that statement. He motioned to a woman to come to pray over me. She began praying in tongues. I never had any faith in this, but suddenly, I was sobbing, and the sobs grew into very heavy, deep crying with water flowing from my eyes, rolling down my cheeks under my chin onto my neck. I had no control over anything. I was too consumed to even be embarrassed. I glowed. Knowing the Lord as we all did, we knew he was washing me clean. It was a beautiful feeling. Everyone praised the Lord with me for the revelation that had happened in my faith. I was no longer depressed. My Spirit was healed.

When I arrived home, I got on my knees alone in my room and stayed on my knees praying for that gift. I was persistent. I promised the Lord I would not get up until I was given the gift to pray in tongues. After about one-half hour or so, I prayed in tongues. "And when the day of Pentecost has fully come, they were all with one accord in one place. And they were all filled with the Holy Ghost, and began to speak with other tongues, as the Spirit gave them utterance" (Acts 2:1, 4, KJV). I only pray in tongues but do not prophesy because I have not been given that gift. I pray on the sick as the Lord leads me to and pray alone in my room as God provides.

*   *   *

Las Vegas, Medifast, and Oprah

As the years passed, I really had run out of steam and took a short time off to coast. In the coasting process, since my husband never supported me financially, I took a temporary job for a very well-known physician who practiced hair transplants. He also was practicing treatment of morbid obese patients with a product called Medifast. He was manufacturing this product in his office, which eventually became a very large business. He was using McCormick products in the mixture, and since I had worked in that department at McCormick for several years during my marriage, I still had contacts there. He liked that idea and used me to his advantage for contacting the proper individuals to help him with the flavors in his product. My competence awarded me with a permanent job as his office manager. I worked at my own pace. He started to do conventions for physicians taking the program to Las Vegas, and he asked me to take the trip with him and his wife and adult children, who were involved in the business, to teach physician assistants in this product for the morbid obese. It turned out to be another walk through the wilderness. I was very instrumental in helping him promote the product to the physicians and their assistants that I was invited back by the national organization the following year. I produced a teaching audiotape that would be distributed to all physicians using the program.

He then had me represent the institute at private events when he couldn't make them. Ironically, one time, he asked me to attend the *People Are Talking* program on TV with Richard Sherr as host and Oprah Winfrey, cohost. I would be called upon in the nutritional portion of the program since the institute was well-known now for the product it was manufacturing.

People Are Talking that day would have two guests. I was there for the second portion, but as God would have it, the following opportunity pursued. The first portion started with a woman who spoke on money management. The subject gradually flowed into talk of the habits of the program's producer in the management of money in her marriage. She was called to the microphone. She and her husband had separate bank accounts. When they bought furniture and things of the house, they would share the financial burden and pay half each for everything.

There was a bit of snickering, etc., and Oprah took a count of hands as to who would *not* be in favor of that arrangement in a marriage. Ninety-nine percent of the audience raised their hands, and my hand came up for the opposite number of 1 percent. I was asked to approach the microphone with Mary, the producer, and explain my thoughts. I was well dressed, looked professional, and simply stated with extreme confidence the *truth* inside of me, expressing words of wisdom: "I just want you to know that I've been married for thirty years and I've worked every single day of my life, and after thirty years, I decided that I needed my freedom, and when I decided to go out and get my freedom, I didn't have a penny of my own money. So actually, I think Mary is doing the right thing."

"Oh," says Oprah, smirking, "so when Mary decides she wants her own freedom, she will have her own money."

And there was lots of laughing, but I pursued, "No . . . no . . . she may never *want* her freedom. The thing is I really never had anything of my own . . . and after thirty years, I wanted it . . . Finally, I didn't own anything. All I owned was *me*."

At this point, the host said, "That is a very good point." I smiled, uprightly raised my first finger, and went to sit down.

It wasn't funny! The act was over, and the audience got the point. I felt good to know that the guest, Carol Colman, had heard of my support of her featured book, *Love and Money*. The host's final comment admitted it was something to think about.

Baltimore taught me much and opened many doors. I never hesitated to walk through them, trusting my faith. I was open to hearing, trying His promises, and eventually making life work for me in His plan. Little did I know what the wilderness had in store for me in the future.

Walk Through the Wilderness

As I walk through the wilderness
to serve you Holy God,
the lamp I carry worthily they see.
Abundantly you set the ground
with fertilizer strong,
the tools you set are ready there
for me.
The seeds I plant at season's time
to watch the fruit then bloom,
are growing into heavy bark,
a tree.
I pray, oh God, these strengthened trees
stay healthy to abound
to know the change of season and
stay free.

Coming Home

The Reason

I made frequent trips home to see the family—mother growing into her late eighties, brother bearing the responsibility with his wife to watch over her, and daughter bearing children, with troubles of her own, now pregnant with her third in four years. The children were beautiful—a son aged three, a daughter aged two, and one soon to be born. An operation had been performed to bring her daughter into the world, and the doctors were predicting that the next one would be born the same way. She called me one day in despair that she just couldn't do this. "Mother, I will never live through it. I have two others here, no money, no help. I won't survive it. Please, Mom, I need help." It was close to her delivery date when they would bring her third, a boy, into the world. I went to the Lord. What could I do? A month earlier, my brother had called to tell me that the family home had been sold and I would be receiving my part of the money. That was a gift from God, which came at the proper time. I could give up work for a while. I needed the rest.

I decided to take a trip home. I was hearing, "Move home, move home, move home." How could I possibly leave this troubled woman I was living with in Maryland and go to my daughter? I prayed, "Lord, please make whatever your plan is possible. I don't know what you have in store for me, in this dilemma." My faith took over. I told my roommate I would be going home to be with my daughter for a short time. I didn't know how long it would be, but I had to answer her call. It would be her responsibility to take care of things in Maryland until I returned.

When I arrived, I found my daughter very distraught. She was crying frequently, and she admitted to me that she had been praying for all these months that God would send her this child normally. In Maryland, I had the opportunity to learn a lot about body healing through massage under the feet called foot reflexology. I made daily visits as I started working under her feet. I really didn't know what I was doing and didn't know whether or not it would work, but my faith through prayer gave me the courage to keep going. For three weeks, every day, my visits showed improvement in her attitude; and she began to feel confident that God would answer her prayer not to have a second cesarean birth. Her doctor said that was the only way she could deliver. The child inside her was standing upright, but with both of us praying to God, asking to hear our request, and manipulating the bottom of her feet, the day before surgery, she called me to come to stay with the children. "I think I am going to deliver." Her water had broken, the child inside her turned, and at 4:00 a.m. the next day, one and a half years after, her daughter Colin was born naturally. I had three grandchildren.

* * *

Another New Beginning

I had found an apartment when I was in Rhode Island and put a deposit on a two-bedroom unit since my roommate, Cindy, was intent on moving with me. I wasn't happy about it, but it was God's will, and I went along with it. She said she was moving with me since she had read the book of Ruth from the Bible.

When I researched the story of Ruth in the Bible, I understood what she meant. From the New American Bible, Catholic 1987 World Bible Publishers, Inc., "the Book of Ruth is named after the Moabite woman who was joined to the Israelite people by her marriage with the influential Boaz of Bethlehem.

"The book contains a beautiful example of filial piety, pleasing to the Hebrews and to Gentiles. Its aim is to demonstrate the divine reward for such piety even when practiced by a stranger. Ruth's piety (Ruth 2:11), her spirit of self-sacrifice, and her moral integrity were favored by God with the gift of faith and an illustrious marriage whereby she became the ancestress of David and of Christ. In this, the universality of the messianic salvation is foreshadowed."

Webster describes *filial* as pertaining to "the generation following the parents." *Piety* means "devoutness toward God."

We were leaving on a very bad day. She was having one of her migraines, and all boxes and furniture were on their way. I was left with all the other work of packing the cars while she kept on with this migraine. Finally, I'd had it. In my boldness, I lost my patience with giving in to an evil thought. "No," said I. "We have prayed those headaches away from you, and I will not accept it. We are leaving here today, and you will be driving your car. You can do it. Don't give in to this, you hear?" It was pouring rain, with thunder and lightning; the weather was treacherous. We were going home through the Pennsylvania mountains, not up Route 95. Didn't know what we would run into. We prayed together before we left, and then we were off! It really was a wild storm. Couldn't see a thing in front of us but fog, and as it got darker, an occasional light here and there. I was praying all the way and kept asking the Lord to clear my vision. She drove behind me in her car. It worked, but there were many trucks on the road that kept passing and splashing our windshields. We were averaging twenty-five miles per hour, and she followed me without a hitch. We had no cell phones on that trip or a GPS; I don't think they were invented yet. We simply trusted God for our destination. After about three hours, we hadn't gone too far, so we prepared to stop in a motel. I stopped at three motels. There were no rooms available until the final stop. Fortunately, a twin-bedded room was available. We checked in, and she was complaining about her migraine. I've never had one, so I really was not patient with all this. However, I said, "I think you will be better once you have eaten something." Well, it worked! After she ate, she said it was gone. We finally lay our heads down on comfortable pillows in a room I hadn't expected, but under the circumstances, it was a castle.

The next morning we woke to absolutely bright sunlight. The storm had passed in the night, and never, considering the condition we were in, did we awake until sunrise. We were anxious to get going. The trip through the mountains was beautiful. It was smooth sailing once we got on the road, finally hitting the East Coast to Route 95 north and on up into Rhode Island by about 6:00 p.m. that day.

Our moving truck arrived the following day. The apartment would be a good temporary place, in a central location of Cranston, near my family and lots of churches. We would have to find jobs, and since we both had cars, it didn't seem we would have to use the bus route that went right by our gate. We had adequate space for all the furniture we had, but I remember that we had to get rid of the piano that had been in my family for many years. The movers explained that they could not transport the piano to the second floor. There was no elevator, and it would be too heavy. Since it had a steel inner body, they were afraid the stairs would not hold the weight.

*　　*　　*

The Churches and the Piano

We had the piano transported to my daughter's house temporarily. Her house was full with three children, and she was very apprehensive of having the piano in her house for too long a period.

One Wednesday night, my roommate and I headed for a church we had heard about. A nice Baptist Evangelical church. By now, it was in the month of November. The weather was beginning to get very cold, and this night, it was after a day of snow falling and settling on the parking lot. There were large patches of ice. My roommate was not too steady on her feet and ended on her derriere. She was extremely miserable by this time since it took us two hours to finally find this church. I was not familiar with the neighborhood, and driving around and around, passing it twice, we found we were only twenty minutes from our apartment dwelling. The next day, after speaking with my daughter, she emphatically asked me to please have the piano removed from her little bungalow. The pressure was on! I had to find some way to get that monstrosity of a piano out of her way.

The following weekend, I posted a notice on the bulletin board advertising the piano for sale. I got a call from the choir director. "Where is the piano? How much do you want for it?" I explained that I would sell it for what it had been evaluated for: $800.00. It was my mother's old upright that had been remodeled and tuned, having all old parts replaced to almost new. He said he would like to see it. So we planned to meet at my daughter's house. When he arrived, he played some very beautiful hymns, and we all joined in singing them. He loved the piano but said he could not buy it. I would be glad to have the piano moved to his house, and he could borrow it until I moved in to another apartment. When I made my change, then I would take it back. He didn't like that arrangement. He would pay for the removal of the piano to his home only if I gave it to him as a gift. He stated that he had been praying for a piano for seven years; his daughter was nine years old, and he wanted her to start piano lessons. His children were young, and he didn't like having to leave the home in the evenings for choir rehearsals. He could have them in the home. How could I resist! I agreed.

He immediately knelt down with his family, thanking God for answering his prayer. He prayed the Lord would bless me and my new life. There I was in the middle of God's faithfulness with my mother's piano. In my mother's aging process, then in her nineties, she never forgot that I had given her piano away. She always seemed to mention in conversation about what I had done. I felt somewhat guilty but kept trying each time to let her understand how happy and grateful this young man was. That she would be in the middle of happiness for this growing family. When I think of the process, I didn't think of what it might do to my mom. All I could think of was how God was using me in the life of this young choir director and his family.

My concern in all was that I never heard from him again. We changed churches, finally going to a church much closer. It too was evangelical. It was a family church. The pastor and wife were very friendly; their grown family, all musicians, ran the music ministry. I was asked to participate with solos from time to time. After a year at that congregation, the old pastor was caught in an affair with the church secretary. He confessed before the church members and was terribly embarrassed as was his whole family. We left, and the church was abandoned.

Many years ago, as we traveled to the beaches, we would pass this very well-known Baptist church. Now back home in Rhode Island, I decided to attend. I liked it. I brought many of my old Catholic friends in Rhode Island to Tuesday night Bible studies. I joined the choir and stayed with the church for three years. Soon, there were rumors about that pastor. He was very young; his wife was beautiful but frail. They were married for a short time, and his wife had just given birth to their sixth child when he was removed from the church. No explanations were given.

I finally tried my daughter's church, the Assembly of God. We did not attend too long when the congregation was moving to get rid of their pastor, whom they had decided was not a good manager in his extravagant financial dealings with his family and the church. All these disappointments with churches had finally put me into an understanding of what I would now be doing. I was coming home, all the way!

Flashbacks

Growing Up in Providence

The youngest of two, I lived on second floor of a six-story tenement house on Ledge Street. It was off Charles Street, in a primarily Italian neighborhood in the north end section of Providence, Rhode Island, with my mom, dad, and my brother. Our paternal grandparent had built it for the family when they arrived in America. My aunt married my father's brother. She was cousin to my mother. They lived next door with seven siblings. Some of them had to eventually sleep downstairs in grandma's tenement. Grandma lived on the first floor, next to the grocery store. She was blind and deaf. She lived with another son and daughter. Aunt Mary became Sister Angela, a nun, at the age of thirty-three. She moved to New York State. I never saw her until I was about ten since she left for the convent when I was eleven months old. She was a musician and taught music in Catholic school at the convent. She died at the age of ninety-two at a nun's retirement home in New York.

Uncle Pat worked as a stonecutter on cemetery stones and eventually died of a lung disease. My mom and Aunt Ma (I called her) took care of Grandmother every day after Aunt Mary left and Uncle Pat's death. Grandmother was our angel. She was never without a rosary in her hand. She prayed for all of us, daily feeling our heights and commenting, "Comme gross" ("how tall" or something to that effect). She would come up the stairs, thirteen of them, and sit in a chair just inside the door of Auntie's or our tenement for the day. We were one big happy family, musically involved, singing in church choir, and ending our days with piano and song.

Grandma died at the age of eighty-two from gangrene in agonizing pain while the church bells were ringing at noon. I was thirteen years of age. I was kneeling on a couch, looking out of the window, listening to the chimes indicating the time, praying that the Lord would take her out of her misery, when suddenly at the end of the ringing, there was complete silence. At that moment, my prayer was answered.

I had pneumonia when I was three. I remember having the same dream, going up a stairway to a curtain that I was scared to enter. I never knew what was beyond that curtain.

It could have meant death, but thank God the Lord didn't need me yet.

My father was the greatest. Before marriage, he traveled with his comedic talent in vaudeville. His father called him home to work in a store. He was a butcher by trade.

He built an open-air theater in our neighborhood, the Continental, where he showed silent films. The oldest girl cousin played the piano to the movies—which indicated tragedy, comedy, and violence with keystone cops—comedians such as Buster Keaton and Charlie Chaplin, and all the women who were old-fashioned beauties in those days. Daddy never got money together to finish the theater by adding the roof before he lost it during the Depression. It was renamed the Columbia. Daddy was kind and gave away what he had to beggars that would come to the door; one of them, Joe "the Millionaire." The Italians in the neighborhood had a warped sense of humor about Joe, with stories poking fun at him, but Daddy felt sorry for him and always gave him money and clothing. Daddy died too young at the age of seventy-six. As a young boy, he smoked cigarettes, which resulted in cranium cancer in his later years. Before he died, he had a twenty-six-piece band. He played the tuba and the bass drum. They were well-known, playing for Italian holidays and church feasts. We always attended. Everybody loved my dad, and so did we.

My mom worked in the Hope Webbing company as a weaver. My brother was four years older than I, and he was made responsible for my drinking my milk every day. Mom was the greatest cook. She was strong. We always heard her story of having been born only one and a half pounds to a very frail mother who died shortly after Mom was born. In her infant days, it was said she was kept in the warm oven as her incubator. Mom was then raised by Aunt Ma's mother on a big farm on Job Street. She found time as a beautiful young lady to take piano lessons and was quite good at it, as I remember.

My brother suffered an illness when he reached eighteen months. It was an infection in his left hip, which resulted in a full body cast every summer for thirteen years to lengthen his shortened leg. Dad set up a showcase in his bedroom where all the kids would go to see movies shown on a blank wall. Those were fun days for all the 65 Ledge Street youngsters growing up on the third floor with our family of nine. My brother graduated the University of Rhode Island and worked for them as their fund-raiser. His trombone playing in many areas of the music world helped get him through college. At the age of eighty-six, he still plays in an all-trombone combo. I was the youngest of the clan, sort of being by myself during those years. I was creative in my thoughts and ideas. I wanted to be an actress.

The Mirror

In a four-room tenement, I was raised.
As one of two, I was stagestruck, crazed.
Although I admit, I wasn't alone,
From my dad, he was vaudeville, I was a clone.
Each morning I'd wake with a creative scheme,
The ideas would flow, to produce my new dream.
I'd slip from the bedroom and step to the left,
On the opposite wall, the mirror was kept.
I dreamed I was Temple, could do what she did.
The judges all watching, in the mirror they hid.
I imagined they thought this child is a find,
We discovered a talent who is one of a kind.
That mirror was magic, I believed what it said,
I performed as my family arose from their bed.
To find that this sibling had what it took.
To produce all her gifts, she'd write in a book.
Now that I'm older, with grands, girl and boys,
We all share together such wonderful joys.
The mirror still judges encouraging feat,
I have to work harder, but goals I still meet.
The energy given from positive visions,
The mirror works with me to make my decisions.
I'm never alone, because God is my bevel,
He straightens my lines to balance my level.
I'll never forsake the mirror, my friend,
My long life I know will now never end.
Eternity promised, must perform as a Saint,
That mirror reflects many pictures to paint.

My family next door were all brothers and sisters to us. Jimmy, the youngest, was only one year older than my brother. Rosalie, the oldest girl, and her brother, Ernest, taught me piano. Rosalie met her mate while visiting her sisters who worked in DC. He had two children from a former marriage, which Rosalie raised. He was from Brazil and worked as the interpreter between President Truman and the president of Brazil. Elsie and Helen had already left home to work in DC. They both married the men they met in DC. Elsie had three children; Helen had none. Lil became a teaching nurse for the Rhode Island Hospital, married a lawyer, and had two children. Edward, the oldest son, married and had three children and was an executive for Procter & Gamble. Ernest became a musician, graduating from the New England Conservatory of Music, and was employed by the Rhode Island Department of Education as a music adviser while he taught piano and voice lessons privately. He married and had one daughter. He and his wife became very important to the Rhode Island Philharmonic Orchestra and Rhode Island Ballet in their volunteer services. Jim, the youngest, went into service, came out, and graduated the University of Rhode Island. He worked for several different companies as an executive. His positions required lots of traveling. He married and had three girls and one boy. All these brothers and sisters I was blessed with are gone now, except for Elsie, who is ninety-two, living with her youngest son, now fifty, in Providence.

*   *   *

My First Vision

Our neighbors living on the third floor were the Cerrones and the Lepores. Eleanor and I were born six days apart. We were close friends. Her mother was from Italy. She had a garden at the top of Windmill Street, right off Ledge Street. She frequently went to the garden, walking up this steep hill, carrying her basket on the top of her head. It was a very normal scene. Many other mothers did that too. Not mine; she was born in America. One day Eleanor and I went with her mother. We were about nine years old. We were sitting on a bench outside of the shack, which was used for gardening chores. Suddenly it began to rain really hard, and there was thunder and lightning. We were covered by an overhang on the shack, so it was exciting when suddenly, in a flash of lightning, I saw a vision of Jesus in the sky. "Eleanor, did you see that?" She asked what, and I told her. She said no. I let go of it, and many years later, actually, after my divorce in my poetry days, I wrote,

Time

It was a long time ago, When lightning hit the skies.
A vision of holiness, It was Jesus in my eyes.
This vision always stayed with me, I only told a few.
Until I felt the comfort, When He called, "I've chosen you."
The years since I have known Him, He's molded me like clay.
To hear His word and teach it, Help others, the Lord's way.
To ready each bright day for Him, I wake and clean my room.
So He can enter in with me, To pray for those in gloom.
And then I sing in thankfulness, In adoration strong.
I dance around and praise Him, An exercise in song.

*   *   *

Mom Takes Her In

One day, my aunt Ma's sister arrived at our house with her five-year-old daughter. She had been the older sister who ran away from home from her overprotective brothers. She lived in New Jersey where she married.

36

Rita was a beautiful little girl, with dark brown banana curls and blue eyes. A little Irish beauty. She was a sort of Shirley Temple (the Temple I refer to in "The Mirror" above), the well-known child movie star. One of her eyes was slightly crossed, but that made no difference to her beauty. After they moved out of our house, they visited us very frequently. Her mom and mine became close buddies, and Rita and I were just two years apart. We enjoyed playing together. We were like sisters. She had no other siblings and consequently stuck very close to her mother. She never married. As this story evolves, Rita becomes a very full part of my life after my marriage, divorce, and return from Baltimore.

*   *   *

Growing Up

I skipped 2B and 4B, which would be the second and fourth grades today. We had school in A and B sections. Anna was a very good friend of mine in school, and she was the smart one. We loved each other and had become such good friends. The teachers thought she should skip those grades, and she wouldn't skip without me. So I skipped too. Which put me one year ahead of myself all the way through high school. I graduated at seventeen years of age.

My acting started in Providence when I was in a radio show with Anna. She played Heidi, and I her friend. As I grew, I became associated with acting groups in school but never felt I was given the roles I wanted. I learned of rejection early in the business of entertainment. I joined Actors Inc., where I played Filumena in *The Rose Tattoo* to rave reviews. Anna Magnani originally played that role in the Italian movie version. Good comedy roles came along in my years after high school into community theater. I loved playing Gooch in *Auntie Mame*, the play at the Barker Players on Benefit Street. It was known in Rhode Island as the oldest community theater in the United States. The acting bug hit me really young, and I just absorbed all that went with it with my own grace and style.

I had a very lovable teacher in fifth grade. She chose me as one of her favorites. Miss O'Neill was unusual. She took four of her favorites on a motor trip one very foggy day. (see epilogue A Fond Memory).

*   *   *

Where It All Started

My goal was to become a nurse, but I never got beyond twelfth grade because of finances. The boy definitely had to have the college education. By the time he graduated, our family funds for education had dried up. That's how it was in those days. I worked in a very exclusive store called TILDEN-THURBER, doing office work; and I was also used in the china and glass departments, cosmetics, and fine jewelry, which taught me the finer things in life. I began to think glamorous. When the Cushman Agency from New York came to Rhode Island to teach a modeling course, I took it. I started modeling locally. I continued piano lessons as I grew older with Sal Fransozzi, the best teacher in those days. He advised me to stop because I was wasting my money. I never practiced when I started dating. I loved creating my own style of playing and enjoyed everything I did on my own anyway. To this day, I am told I make that piano "talk."

I worked for doctors. I worked for a dentist as his office manager and assistant. He taught me to clean teeth, and I worked as a hygienist before it was completely illegal. I had to stop when they became licensed. I started to surprise a lot of people with the kind of things I did in my growing days. I joined the International Institute and took part in many of their functions. My cousin Edward got me involved in that. I really looked up to my oldest cousin because he and I acted in plays together. We played opposite each other in *The Matchmaker*, the play version of the musical, *Dolly*. He was a wonderful actor and did summer stock.

I joined the Players, Actors Inc., where I played the lead role in *The Rose Tattoo*, a drama set in Italy where the husband was blown up in his own truck. She thought he was selling bananas. I was active with the Barker Players in Providence for many years. They named themselves the oldest community theater in the country, but when I got to Baltimore, the Vagabonds disputed that statement. I never went beyond that conversation.

And then one summer, eight years after I graduated high school, I met my mate. He had just graduated Brown University, was from Newport, and had an apartment in Providence. We met in October and married in May. I was just short of twenty-five years of age, and he was thirty.

Back In Rhode Island

The Cocktail Lounge

It was a cocktail lounge where people would sing around the piano, something I was very used to doing in my heavy partying and theater days. I found a few cousins there and an old girlfriend of mine I'd met at the Players that night. I joined them at their table. I ordered cranberry juice while the others drank hard liquor. Before entering the building, I sat in my car and prayed, "Lord, if there is anyone here who needs to hear from you, use me, just speak through me." While sitting with the group, I noticed a man who was standing at the bar who turned his head in my direction. He was large, not attractive, with a protruding abdomen and a look of deep sadness, like many others hanging in and around the bar. He motioned to me to come to him. I excused myself and joined him at the bar. No one actually even knew I left the table.

When I walked up to him, I stood at his right. Suddenly, I felt this feeling going through me like I was glued to the floor. I could not move in any direction. He said to me, "You looked like the only person in this room that I can talk to," and I will never forget what I said to him. My words were "I am." Jesus spoke through me. The man began to tell me that he felt the devil was after him. He was holding a large brandy snifter with a good deal of brandy in it. He opened himself up to me by explaining that he had a girlfriend that he was living with for years. She had just become a born-again Christian and would have to change her life with him. He told me he loved her and would abide by her requests. Her sister was the devil in the plan, he said. She was interrupting their settling plans by demanding that they separate. I listened to this long story. I still could not move. My feet were glued to the floor. Finally, I said, "It isn't the devil that is after you. It is Jesus. Those spirits that you are holding in your hand do not belong to God. It is His spirit calling you. You told me that you used to sing opera, and now when you sing, you use strange words that you do not recognize. You are singing in tongues, like in the book of Acts in the Bible." He said that his girlfriend told him the same thing. He turned away from me, but my feet were glued to the floor and I still could not move.

He began to talk to the man next to him on the other side, ignoring me. Suddenly, he turned toward me again, looked straight into my eyes, put his brandy glass down on the bar, and said, "Good-bye, you will never see me in here again." I was released and went back to my chair.

*   *   *

Not Missing the Train

Once, I was waiting for a train to pick me up from a small local station in Massachusetts. I had just attended an audition for a commercial. I noticed a man looking around the money meters. I imagined he was looking for change for his next cup of coffee. He looked like a homeless man, and he was bothering no one. I dug into my purse and found a dollar. He had turned away and was starting to walk up the hill from the station. I was afraid I would miss the train, but my spirit made me follow this man. I felt I couldn't reach him. He was a bit ahead of me, and my body wasn't moving fast enough to catch up. And when I did, it was at the end of the street, on the top of an incline. I quickly tapped him on the shoulder, when he turned toward me. I said, "Here, take this." He said, "Why are you giving me this? You are kind." And I said, "You were not begging, so I am giving." I quickly turned around, hoping I had not missed my train, took two steps, and quickly turned to see where he would be going, and he was not there. I looked in every direction, and he had literally disappeared.

Another time, at the train station at Back Bay, Boston, it was a cold winter evening. There was a lady sitting on a milk crate, sort of huddled in the warmth of her own body. She was not begging, so I went over to her with a five-dollar bill. I gave her the money and told her she should go into the station, get warm, and get herself something to eat. She looked at me and said, "May God bless you." I then said to her, "Would you promise me please not to spend this on alcohol?" (She really looked like she might be an alcoholic.) Her very sad, tired eyes looked at me and said, "I promise I will try." So I left her to God.

* * *

Some Acting Successes

HEIGHT: 5'6" DRESS: 10-12 HAIR: GRAY EYES: BROWN

In 1991, soon after I returned to Rhode Island, I was looking for something to do. I had always wanted to be in a pageant in my young days but never had the opportunity or money to enter the competition. Well, I finally entered one. The Miss Rhode Island senior pageant. I won and had the opportunity to go to nationals in Atlantic City paid by the Buttonwoods Senior Center.

I guess God knew He had instilled in me the gift of teaching. I was successful in teaching Brown University's learning community, a workshop in acting for television and film, the Learning Connection, and Rhode Island College's theater association. The critics were healthy from the students and my supervisors who were present to observe my work.

In 1995, I was cast in a commercial for Kraft cheese, which paid me residuals in the amount of $25,000. The commercial ran for a period of one and a half years. My daughter, living in their first home with the three children, needed a new roof, a new heating unit, furniture, and other large items that did my money justice. I did manage to take a trip to Minnesota to visit a cousin, who in turn insisted I take a few days for myself. She introduced me to complete luxury at the Aveda health spa at that time in Wisconsin for three days and two nights. A wonderful interlude, alone, in a terry cloth robe, in snowy cold country in the month of November, eating healthy and experiencing massages, essential oil baths, facials, beauty treatments, manicures, and pedicures. That was by far one of the best vacations I ever had.

*　　*　　*

Being Christ's Ambassador

This morning, I was summoned to visit my friend Evelyn's house where they would be playing cards in the afternoon. I went because her dear friend is living with a long bout of cancer. She is *living* with it: gets out to play cards, cooks for guests at her home—her passion—with her bald head due to chemo, pain in her body, and this day in her chest, but *living*.

I walked in at the appointed time. The game was ending. We visited for what seemed moments, but God had turned it into His timing. We were all standing, and they were getting ready to leave when I asked Evelyn if she had any olive oil. She looked at me kind of funny, said she did, and produced it. I poured a drop into the cover, and Mary, our dear friend in pain, glowed. I told her I was going to bless her with the oil and pray over her. None of the others were aware of what was going on. It seemed that they were distracted by a conversation away from us. Suddenly, the prayer flowed from me into her right ear as I touched her. I made the sign of the cross on her forehead and chest with the oil as she clutched the cross, which dropped from the rosary beads she was clutching around her neck. She isn't even Catholic! She looked into my eyes and thanked me. I had acted in obedience.

They left for home, which would be a three-fourth-hour drive. She called me as soon as she got home. She reported that the pain left her chest halfway home and she would now lie down to rest.

The reading for that day from Charles Stanley's *In Touch* magazine was Isaiah 6:1-8: "We are Christ's ambassadors to a hurting world and there are varied reactions to our presence. God wants us to live out our faith in the workplace, our communities and at home, regardless of others' reactions. We must ask ourselves . . . Has my faith permeated the many areas of my life?"

* * *

The Front-store Church

I was invited to present some of my poetry in a front-store church that the two pastors, Linda and Ken Hudson, had started. My presentation would be to young mostly black families happy to be together in fellowship, praise and worship, and lots of goodies that these families had baked or the pastors had bought. It was a joy to be there. They were happy to be in this warm environment where they were accepted and their children were open to being entertained by an author of short stories and myself. When I walked in, the author was in the middle of one of his stories. The audience was completely involved in the story itself, and they were responding to every action within the story taking place. I also became very much involved. Being an actress myself, I was surprised that in spite of the fact that the author had no acting ability and was somewhat more blaze than I would have been in the action script, the points were made to great understanding and provided great entertainment for all in attendance.

When I got up to perform with some of my poetry, I involved all the children to become part of my presentation. I read poems that were teaching good morals and truth, which is my style, and included the children to become part of the material. I acted one poem out, "Sniffles," in the middle of the "flu" season, which included rants and snorts and an argument with God, who finally told me to "be calm and spend this time upon a psalm and get back into bed with the hot water bottle at my head." I received the joy that evening among people who showed great appreciation for the time we spent with them. Poets and writers like myself have so much to share. We may never be published, but what we have to share is true love that comes from the heart. Each one of us with our own unique gifts. These unique gifts should be given away. Let us help more individuals to be able to sit down and let go of their emotions in poetry, prose, and stories; for when the words are written down, the author cleanses and the recipients may become richer in spirit. After all, the Ten Commandments were written in stone. This prompted me into becoming a member of the Rhode Island Short Story Club, which at this writing is 115 years old. Our first anthology was printed in 2007.

*   *   *

My Family

Of course, my brother had lost his first wife, Beverly, to cancer after six years of their marriage long before I had moved to Baltimore. Their only child, Judy, then four, came to live with me for some time and grew up as sister to David, my firstborn. It was difficult to leave her back in Rhode Island when we moved to Baltimore, but my brother didn't think he wanted her to move away from him and my mom, who eventually took over the job. She was aging, but when Judy was thirteen, my brother remarried Marion, who was bringing her five-year-old, Nancy, into the marriage. He adopted her. During the twenty-five years that I lived in Baltimore, Judy had graduated the University of Rhode Island, married, and became a professor at Johnson & Wales University. She always considered me her closest relative, as mother to her in her growing years. Her marriage has been a good one. She married a divorced man with two young children. She raised the children and put her husband through college. He also now is a professor at Johnson & Wales. Tommy's marriage to Marion lasted forty years, when he lost her to ALS in 2004.

*   *   *

45

Mother and the Nursing Home

We gave Mom a wonderful ninetieth birthday party in 1991 and another at one hundred. She seemed in good health even at that age. She lived alone in subsidized housing, and I began to spend a lot of time with her in my freedom. She had a fall, which eventually put her into assisted care, living in a very nice nursing home where she was well cared for. She almost lived to the age of one hundred and two. Her last days were quiet and peaceful, gracefully passing away in the middle of the night (see epilogue One Hundred Years Passed).

*　　*　　*

Aunt Angie

She was my mother's sister. She lived alone after the passing of her husband in North Andover, Massachusetts. She was in her late eighties, near ninety, when I called her to come to visit and stay with me while she visited her sister. They hadn't seen each other for years. The weekend she was to visit, she ended up in the hospital, where her doctor suggested she do something about getting rid of the large home and moving close to whomever could oversee her aging years.

I found the Pocasset Lodge in Rhode Island, where she finally moved in to Independent Living quarters. She was able to see her sister frequently. I was writing my poetry book at that time, *Into the Spirit: A Poetic Witness*, and my aunt gave me $600 and made me promise I would have it published. It was enough money to have two hundred copies printed by a publisher. I gave away most of them, but the bookselling for $5.00, which didn't give me all that much money, I was able to donate to Cindy in her poverty-stricken state. And since then, I have opened an educational fund for my grandson's future education. Since it was just a chapbook, I took it apart from the staples, and I began reprinting them myself and kept giving them away. The last one hundred I had copied, some I sold, but the ones I gave away I paid for myself. Caleb's fund is well on its way; however, the cost of Catholic educational facilities these days are prohibitive. I will need to sell lots of these books in order that we have adequate funds to see that he is properly educated regarding the plans that God has for his life.

She was two years younger than my mom, and they both died within two years of each other after a few grateful years together.

*   *   *

My Other Family

I arrived home to find my cousin Elsie aging. She had lost her job. It was only a temporary job as a senior employee. The family home she and her son were living in was sold by her siblings. They went to live in a home that was left to her by a man friend whom she nursed during his fatal illness. He left it to her in his death. It wasn't much of a place, and still isn't, but she had to move somewhere. She had no other place to go. Now, twenty years later, they are still struggling in that home that needs new wiring, tightened windows, new heating system, a kitchen cooking stove, bathroom fixtures, paint, and more. He was a good son with a warm heart and appreciated all his mother did for him during his complete breakdown for twenty years previous as a recluse. I did all I could to help him tend to his mom, who is now ninety-two, as he holds on to a temporary job with Walmart. He drives an unsafe car back and forth to work, approximately thirty or more miles a day, depending on whether he works early before his mom is out of bed. On those days, he goes home at lunch and feeds her a nourishing meal to last her until he arrives home again after work. I spent many years assisting both of them and only realize now that I myself am aging and am leaving the help up to God. My heart aches that I am not able to assist him in all his responsibilities, much of them financial. There isn't any other family in a position to be helpful, and it seems that in his business to survive, he has not been able to find the proper help that may be available to him in this challenge. She is blind and has lost a lot of her zest and just sits and waits for him to come home. She was so good to my mom when I was away all those years.

The rest of her family was busy helping an elder sister, Helen. She was being directed by the rest of her siblings, deciding a life and place for her in her state of early dementia. Watching this process brought some grief and separation into the family for several years. There was nothing anyone could do since in her good days. Helen had made specific appointments to her estate. I prayed for the Lord to intervene and be merciful with the outcome. It was His call. Helen was called home in a very unhappy ending. Two of her brothers and one sister followed shortly afterward, leaving Elsie, the only survivor in that family. She has life with God on earth. She, like our blind grandmother, sits and waits with her rosary beads in hand.

*   *   *

International Society of Poets

I had never heard of this society. I do think I was contacted because of my publication, *Into the Spirit, A Poetic Witness*, my chapbook. Anyway, it was a very inspirational convention with the International Society of Poets. We all were able to recite our poems to judges, and they voted on the presentations. It was an educational adventure. I was alone at this convention in Washington, DC. There were over four hundred people there from all over the world.

The convention progressed, and at the last banquet before we left, a small number of us were awarded monetary gifts for our poems. It was a $50 check. My poem was "The Kingdom Award." After the banquet, a bunch of people met at the cocktail lounge, many of whom I'd never met. We seemed to only get to meet people at nearby tables only. I wasn't drinking at all at that time and hesitated to go into the cocktail lounge, but God was kind. I was drawn to a bunch from England, Ohio, and others who spoke English. There was a piano player who was engaged for the evening, played very well, and so I joined him at the piano with my vocal ability. He was pleased, playing normal songs, of course, that we all knew.

This Linda from Ohio was a real gatherer. I guess she thought I was hired with the piano player, and she came over to me and told me she was with a person who sang gospel real well and wondered if the player knew "Amazing Grace." He said no; he had never heard of it. I said I had and was a piano player and, if he'd let me sit down, I would play it for her. I don't think I ever saw a piano player move off the bench so fast. It was incredible. I'll never forget it. It was an act of God. Linda was ecstatic, and so was I. Her friend did have a beautiful voice, sang in the key of C, which was a cinch for me, and we were off.

All of us seemed to be in one accord. It was a night at this cocktail lounge for God's people to show off with his kind of music. Linda and her friends from Ohio were super people, and the foreigners that gathered among us were familiar with God's music; we were the league of nations. The piano player never came back, so we stayed there singing with great joy and music, voices and song. We really rocked, praising the Lord like a bunch of Christians can, which prompted the waitress to come to us afterward to tell us, "This place never had such life in it, at least not since I've been working here."

Linda and I have stayed friends for ten years now. At one point about five years ago, she had a book of poems published by someone she met at that convention from Stibington, England. I am published in that book. It is called *Poetry and Praise*.

*   *   *

A Spiritual Boost

Larry, a good friend I met in 1997 during the musical production of *Rage of the Heart*, who was about to start his own Christian newspaper, *Good News in RI*, referred me to someone he had met at a Baptist church. Samuel had moved to Wickford, Rhode Island, recently to retire from his business as an editor in New York for many years. Larry knew I had been writing and our networking had been in overdrive.

In my search for more confidence and knowledge, I went to the church to make it a point to meet Samuel. I did. At a service, I made it my business to attend with Larry one Sunday. At a social get-together after that service, I gave him my phone number and asked him to contact me when he might have some time to discuss my poetic gifts. During a luncheon meeting with him, he commented on the poetry of William Blake, comparing my "The Kingdom Award" to Blake's "The Tiger," written from a divine nature. "Indeed you should keep on with your work. There's a point of diminishing returns, however, in my ability to help. Insofar as your inspiration is divine [like Blake's], and as you have little time to devote to the mundane [revision, revision, revision], accordingly, I take off my editor's hat—and pray for you." To say the least, after follow-up with a copy to him of my *Into the Spirit, A Poetic Witness*, now in its third printing since 1998, he insisted on paying me for it with congratulations.

I had many thanks to offer up for that experience. One in which I could never have engineered myself. They always seem to be the ones that lead down the path God is overseeing. This gave me the courage to press on to the point of getting all this in print. Praise the Lord.

Changing Times

Going It Alone

I had been living with Cindy for five years. My spirit was tired. I needed rest from caregiving again. Cindy had lost her job. We survived the move to Rhode Island together, but the time had come to separate. I felt burdened and smothered. I openly discussed with her that many years had lapsed and there needed to be a change in our arrangement. I needed my privacy. I allowed my spirit to guide me all the way. I just had to listen and be obedient and carry through what I was hearing, or I would collapse. It seemed this was a pattern in my life—to get to a point where I had done all I could do from the power within me and then I have to let go. The human portion of me becomes tired, and the spirit needs renewal. Fortunately, I do renew the spirit, am given that new energy, and the next door is opened at the given time.

I had heard of a Christian facility in Chicago that would help Cindy. She learned of it at the same time. I suggested she look into going there for help. She agreed, and it worked. I took an apartment, alone. With God's guidance, it all worked out right for both of us. I found a part-time job as a legal secretary to help me pay the rent. I immediately went out to apply for subsidized housing and was notified that there would be a two- or three-year wait. I prayed during those years that I would be provided with an apartment with the same charm that our second luxury apartment had. Of course, I knew it would have to be smaller and not as luxurious. I prayed for first floor, with white tile in the hall and kitchen, with a sliding door onto a concrete patio. The Lord was faithful. I had purchased a used piano, and it fit perfectly on a living room wall. It was a very comfortable and serene environment with a road where many geese, ducks, and other animals came walking with their families daily.

On my own, I was free to be me. By now, I was back in my birthright—Catholic church. I eventually changed churches close to my moves, which gave me the comfort of spirit for many reasons. I really knew God by this time and knew of His love and glory. I knew He was everywhere with everyone, and I was the one to choose my friends and share what I knew about Him. He had taught me that the church was within me, not the building or religiosity. I was finally at home. I attended church where my children had baptism and communion. I always liked that church. One Sunday, there was a notice in the bulletin announcing the need for CCD instructors. I immediately applied and chose the sixth graders and asked the leader if I could work from Bibles. Of course, he agreed. I began teaching as each student became familiar on using the Bible and learning about the love of God and the gifts of the Holy Spirit from Galatians 5:22. I taught there for two consecutive years. Sixth graders are not easy to teach, especially the boys, but I know I had some impact on some of the students and left the tougher ones to God.

Cindy finally arrived back from her hospital in Chicago, attended another Evangelical church, and found a middle-aged married couple that took her in and assisted her in getting all the benefits she needed to survive in a comfortable living condition. Her doctors had diagnosed her and recommended Medicaid and Social Security. At this writing, she is living in comfortable housing and gives back as God allows. She has completely given up the idea of ever moving back to Maryland where her sister and brothers still live. She does, however, visit them occasionally. As in the book of Ruth, Cindy fulfilled her spirit of self-sacrifice and her moral integrity and her devoutness toward God; and through her trust in Him, God's reward led her to a woman and her husband, whom she met in her church, who were ready to accept a new responsibility together with the love from within Cindy's heart, which eventually strengthened each one's faith.

As I look back, it is interesting to see how the Lord works. He plans the moves of his workers and the steps of their receivers to a simple good end. He prepares the lives of his followers with change. Each change becomes more exciting and more challenging. Psalm 36:11 says, "If they obey and serve Him, they shall spend their days in prosperity, and their years in pleasures." It is not an easy task to wait upon the Lord. Some days you think you will never live out the day, but the Lord within you can do great things. Ask me; I know.

*   *   *

Two Traumatic Worldly Events

One was the death of Princess Diana of England. The whole world experienced trauma since she was so loved. I, for one, responded with a poem, obtained an original stamp from England in her honor, and affixed it to the poem. I hold that as a memory and give out copies to anyone requesting them. There were only a limited number of stamps, I believe, at that time, so I retain the original.

*   *   *

DARK TUNNELS
by Edna Panaggio

A princess so beautiful and white
whose love transcended all she'd meet
envisioned motherhood, and bride so white
changed blackened outline, interrupted feat.

Her prince left..bringing darkness into play
to turn this unearned tunnel black.
Events of life encountered day by day,
to cover each enlightened crack.

A final tunnel waiting dark and dim,
not ever seen by blinded eye.
The ending darkness turned to scrim,
eternal soul in death to join the spirit sky.

Dark Tunnels

A princess so beautiful and white
whose love transcended all she'd meet,
envisioned motherhood, and bride so white
changed blackened outline, interrupted feat.
Her prince left, bringing darkness into play
to turn this unearned tunnel black.
Events of life encountered day by day,
to cover each enlightened crack.
A final tunnel waiting dark and dim,
not even seen by blinded eye.
The ending darkness turned to scrim,
eternal soul in death to join the spirit sky.

*   *   *

9/11

Don't we all remember it so clearly? I was led to intercessory prayer at that time. A pamphlet came to my spirit and haunted me to create it. I felt it as a divine appointment, and in the Lord's sense of humor with me, it is called God's emergency fast-food weapon against destruction. "It is up to us to save the universe." He knows me well. I do respond! On the inside it describes spiritual warfare and how to pray. Romans 8:26 says, "In the same way, the spirit helps us in our weakness. We do not know what we out to pray for, but the Spirit himself intercedes for us with groans that words cannot express." Ephesians 6:10-19 is referring to the armor of God as we use it for our protection. It also describes a Psalm given to me, which cries out to God for our salvation. These are sent out with my books to purchasers. The back of this creative pamphlet holds a message given to my Holy Spirit from what I assume to be from the spirits of those called by God on September 11, 2001.

Our Spirit's Lament

I thought it was a dream, so bad, I couldn't scream.
Cruel faces acting crimes, shed blood using special knives.
The sun, a blinding light, twin towers were in sight,
When suddenly we hit, hijackers in the cockpit.
We all became a maze, God saved us in a daze.
All spirits came alive, to live this fearful drive.
Oh, dear ones, how you grieve, the sights you can't believe.
Our bodies you can't find, transformed a different kind.
We're working now from here. Those culprits that you fear
Cannot survive the groans, that come from our God's throne.
Their deaths will be satire, they'll end in burning fire.
Your work on earth's begun, dear mortals, God's love,
Unite as one.
If you don't go God's way, you're just as bad as they.
The world will never be, the world God wants to see.
Destruction then will come, will be the end for some.
Don't know what God will do, God Bless, we'll pray for you.

*   *   *

Evelyn at 22 Oaklawn Avenue

During those years in the luxurious apartment together, on one Saturday morning, I met Evelyn. She was preparing for her last daughter to enter college and was steadily packing the car with belongings that would be surrounding her, supposedly, for the next four years. Evelyn would then be alone in this three-bedroom apartment that had been her home where she lost her husband. Two other daughters were well situated into their careers. Now she would be alone in this large apartment.

Evelyn herself had a very interesting background, and I learned of it as we became very close friends. After her graduation from Emerson College, she lived a very exciting career working for station WEEI in Boston, where she interviewed 1940 celebrities—Louis Armstrong, Ella Fitzgerald, Rodgers and Hammerstein, Leonard Bernstein, Glenn Miller, Benny Goodman, Sid Caesar, and Zero Mostel. She had encountered Kate Smith, Cole Porter, Arthur Godfrey, and Emmett Kelly. It has been recently quoted by the Barrington Public Library, where she recently appeared with her adventures that "she will focus on her celebrity adventures in New England's biggest city during the nation's biggest war."

We had many good times together as she included my interests in hers when we attended and became members of the ARTS programs in Cambridge. We would take the train up on "performance" days, stop in the soup spot next door for lunch, and before boarding the train for home, we would find an interesting restaurant for dinner. We learned to drink our warm water together, split meals, and one particular time, I remember splitting a glass of wine, asking for two glasses. Our personalities did not clash; we had fun.

I knew her as a real dear friend, when one day, we had tickets with reservations to attend the Players in Providence to see *Steel Magnolias*. It was a 2:00 p.m. performance on Sunday. That morning, I had a call from a union member informing me that the production company filming *Other People's Money* with Danny DeVito and Gregory Peck would be selecting extras to spend three nights in Connecticut—hotel etc. paid, union scale. As we were driving to the east side, I mentioned my call but turned it down because of my promise to Evelyn. She immediately said, "Turn the car around, you are going to Connecticut." I was amused, and she insisted it wasn't funny. I went to Connecticut, came home after three days and nights working on the movie, learning to eat Thai food and making over $700. Now that's a friend I would say. I mention the fact that Evelyn was another Jewish friend I met in my new acquaintances since returning to Rhode Island. God brought me back to my roots, and He was including many of his so-called chosen people. At age ninety-one, Evelyn was making celebrity status once again through the library performances, another one next week at Rochambeau Library in Providence's east side where I would film it. She gave me this great big introduction as her dear actress friend and videographer. She has turned out to be a very sincere friend.

*   *   *

Temporary Legal Secretary

During the next few years, I continued with the life that I had to share with those around me. The stories continued to evolve. The Lord seemed to free me to my new experiences.

I met a woman that would be working as a temporary secretary, as I was, in a very large law firm. She came to me out of the blue as if she knew me and told me she understood I was divorced. She was concerned with many questions. I had never seen her before, which seemed very strange to me. She explained her rich husband wanted her out and was working toward leaving her with nothing. I didn't know anything about law or what she was talking about; all I knew was that her husband of thirty years was not being very considerate about where she would be going. Well, I took it upon myself to involve some spiritual assistance and promised that I would pray for her and I was sure that everything would be worked out to her benefit. She told me that she would be appearing in court with her husband and his "sharp" lawyer in four days. That her lawyer had listened to her plea to approach his lawyer to convince him that she was in need of some consideration; however, her lawyer betrayed her and went over to the other side, taking the part of her husband.

The day of her court date had arrived. I had put her into very deep prayer. I had quickly done some research in the Bible with regard to her situation and had written a letter to her husband's lawyer, quoting from the Bible some very strong words against what he would be doing. They were word for word from the Bible. I did not sign it. She never knew; I followed God's law, to be silent, and there would be a victory in progress. I told her she need not fear. The Lord would have his angels surrounding the courtroom, and Jesus would be with her and would never leave her until the end of the session.

The day after her court date, she came right over to me. She said, "You will never know what happened." The case was not going too well, and she was beginning to panic when suddenly the door to the courtroom swung open. Everyone became concerned that the door was opened and there was no one entering. During all the confusion about the door, she confided in me that it was then that she realized Jesus had joined the courtroom scene. She completely relaxed, knowing that he was then present and everything would be done in the favor of God. In the final outcome, she was awarded the summer home and many other large things that had been disputed upon. That following summer, I was invited to join her in her summer home for a week's vacation. Romans 8:28 says, "We know that all things work for good for those who love God, who are called according to His purpose."

*　　*　　*

Meeting Marie

I met Marie and had a few great years of friendship. She lived in Attleboro, had a cottage on the Cape, and shared her wonderful personality with us. Marge, another friend of mine, had met her at a counseling service where both had lost their mates, one to divorce and one to death. She and Marge traveled a lot together. I couldn't afford it until one time she and I went along with a group traveling to Arizona on an Elder Hostile in the rainy season. It was truly an experience.

When she moved to Florida, we would get together when she came home to the Cape in the summer months. In Florida, she went through a periodic colonic exploration of her health, which resulted, accidently, in her death just two years ago. At the burial, I was asked by her family to give tribute, and I gave a reenactment of the story of our experience with the Arizona travel to California in a horrible storm. All who attended enjoyed the story, which showed her personality of love and joy and the gifts she was given through the love of God. (see epilogue The Commuter Plane)

*   *   *

The Modeling School

My time at the law firm had ended. I consulted the employment pages and found that a modeling school was looking for instructors. I had all the experience that was needed, with several references from Maryland that I had worked for. I actually was overqualified, with all the experience as an acting union member from 1984 and all the film work that I had done and continued to do when I moved back to Rhode Island. I had more qualifications than any one of the other instructors. And of course, I was the oldest too.

I had many good years with the owner. She was a good businesswoman with scruples, good ones. She was dedicated to her franchise with John Casablancas Modeling and Career Centers. We had dedicated students who wanted to learn and become actors. Certain young hopefuls would come to me, as one of their instructors, and ask for extra help for entering pageants, etc., and I was happy to give all I had to them without compensation so that their dreams would be met. I became very involved with two pageant reps working for the Miss USA system, which eventually appointed me as one of their judges. I naturally helped each pageant entrant from the school to be their best on the runway. At the time, I was working with a skin care and makeup line. One particular really interested and definite student dedicated toward her goal was Claudia. Upon winning Miss Rhode Island, I called her to congratulate her and made an appointment to support her by going to her home, meeting her lovely family, taught her the system with my products, and gave her a whole gift of the skin products and encouragement to go forth and be a good example to the industry in her quest for Miss USA. She evidently followed it through. She never made Miss USA, but someone along the line picked up this beauty; and I have seen her reaching her goal on *The Price is Right* as a model, *Deal or No Deal* as box no. 1 holder in the line of beauties, and just recently, spokesperson for the Miss USA pageant for Donald Trump. There were others. I loved my work.

Then one day, that segment came to an end with the owner and her husband, who were together in the business. He never showed up too much during those years. They were young when they met. She went through the divorce without my even realizing all this was happening. I am one to stay away from anyone else's business unless the Lord forces me into his territory. I had left for a year's time-out since I never was a full-time worker because of my health, and during that time, she gave the business to her husband in the divorce.

When he took over, he called me to go to work for him. I did. I found that he really had no business being the proprietor of a modeling school for young men and women. Here I was in the middle of an employer not qualified to be running a school for young people. I had to stay until I couldn't stand it any longer. He didn't like my boldness, and so he asked me to leave. It was a mistake on his part he knew. My students, their parents, and the modeling community have a lot of respect for me, so he called me back. Shortly afterward, he fired me again because he and I just couldn't see eye to eye on important things that he considered not so important. He called me in after that, apologized for letting me go, and wanted me back. I told him I would never work for him again. He needed the Lord. Christmas rolled around, and I went in to see him with a package—a Bible wrapped neatly. I asked to speak with him at which time he welcomed me into his office. We discussed the Lord. I gave him the Bible, said I would keep him in prayer, and asked him to take this seriously. He needed salvation. He kissed me on the cheek, thanked me for my concern, and wished me a merry Christmas.

That summer, I was walking through the shopping mall, and I heard someone call my name. He was standing by the counter where he was drinking a cup of coffee. He called me over.

He told me that I had given him the best gift he had ever received. That because of my gift of a Bible, he had turned to the Lord and was born again. He was no longer drinking or taking drugs and found that everything was different in his life since his search for God. He had sold the school after realizing that what I had told him all along was right. God had spoken to him to confirm it. Psalm 4:8-9 says, "But you have given my heart more joy than they have when grain and wine abound. In peace I shall both lie down and sleep, for you alone, Lord, make me secure."

*   *   *

Talent America

A student from the modeling school came to me when she saw an ad on TV from a Talent America. She wanted to compete in the talent and modeling portions to see if she would qualify for a trip to the big-time New York. Students seemed to have faith in my decisions for them, and so did their parents. Talent America is a talent-and-models-search company, which brings young people with their parents to the next plateau where they are seen by New York agents. I met the husband-and-wife team that ran this very nice organization, and because of my background, I was asked to be their Rhode Island director.

At that time, I was living in subsidized housing and met the mailman, who told me he had a daughter that never stopped singing at home. She was five years old. I suggested she compete in Talent America. She came to New York three consecutive times as she grew from child, youth, then to teen categories. She won top place for all three competitions. This year she will be entering Berklee School of Music in Boston, Massachusetts, and has already performed in professional theater and musical concerts of her own.

I had fifteen great years as director for the Eastwoods. Met lots of nice agents in New York that were important to my career. I was selected Talent America Director of the Year in 1997. Those were wonderful years, which took me to competitions for talent every July where I stayed in the most exclusive hotels in New York. The competitions for the models were always in Stamford, Connecticut, at the Marriott. My job was to search for talent in the Rhode Island area, take care of all their needs at conventions, and provide guidance for the young contestants. Competitors came from other parts of the country with talent directors, representing their states.

Those conventions once a year were exciting. I got to see lots of good Broadway shows and meet some interesting people. A young singer at age eleven, who won one year from my Rhode Island's contestants in New York because of our encouragement, attended and graduated Berklee School of Music and has cut her first CD in Nashville, Tennessee. Lots of our people have moved on up into top billing throughout the country and abroad. All were lovers and followers of Christ. It seemed that God was always present where his gifted individuals gathered.

*   *   *

The World Premiere

I taught an acting workshop in East Greenwich, where I met a young man. He had a brother who had been a priest but had left the priesthood because of his ingenious talents in the area of composing musicals based on cultural principles. He was a composer, lyricist, playwright. His brother insisted I meet him, and as God would have it, I became involved with his dream (see epilogue The Musical is Born in Divine Providence).

During this time, I met Lou. He was looking for something big to promote. We met through an ad for Talent America that I had put into the paper. When that something "big" came up, I called him and he and I pulled the people together to produce a world premiere at the Veterans Memorial Auditorium in Rhode Island. His wife was leaving him; he was devastated, and so the Lord used me to encourage and guide him into servanthood. He was in his early forties. *Rage of the Heart* opened in April 1997.

*   *   *

My Cousin Rita

My cousin Rita had finally lost all her family and was left alone. She had lived a very sheltered life with her mother. Her last relative they lived with was being buried, and I was attending the service. That morning, I was in prayer, as I always am, on my knees and experienced a wave of realization that she would be asking me to live with her. I argued with God. If this is you, she will ask me herself; but I didn't think she would, really. I was wrong. After the burial service, a very few people attended breakfast with her, and she came to me immediately to plan the rest of her life. She said she had been left enough money to care for the both of us. She is two years older than I. I truly hesitated. I gave her all the pros and cons, but in her fear of being alone, she insisted that she couldn't handle it. Here I was again in the middle. "Oh, God, this business about obedience." I know God understood me and where I was going, but in my submission, I usually have a bout with Him. He knows me so well. But by that time, I had some time to myself. I was living in subsidized housing for three years, alone, and loved it. Before that, after Cindy, I lived alone in a basement apartment in Warwick. So it was time again, and God would have His way with me.

So I taught her new things. She had made her communion and confirmation together at thirteen but never went to church. She began to attend with me. She attended my Bible studies at home and outside of the home with Christian friends I had met and later at St. Rocco's Catholic Church Bible studies. I took her to Charismatic/Evangelical meetings, where she accepted the Holy Spirit.

We went back to luxury apartment living; eventually, I suggested she buy a condominium and, at the same time, buy investment property. My cousin has been an angel in my life. She is part Irish, an only child, but her mother delivered a stillborn son before she was born. My Irish son-in-law and their children became family to her. The investment property became a rental for their family at a very nominal monthly payment so that they could save money to eventually purchase it. The purchased part of it never worked out, however. There were no savings. I provided a life for her that she never dreamed of. She had lived a very sheltered life, never married, never managed her own life.

She was a retiree from the Outlet Company and never went back to work after that. Her supervisor, during her years of service with the Outlet Company, remained a good friend. Lee had moved to Florida, and since Rita was so scared to fly, I encouraged her that it would be fine to visit Lee since God was opening up new things to her so we need not worry. We would have a safe flight and many more of them in the future. She would never travel alone.

*　　*　　*

Our Florida Vacations and Synagogue

The first trip was spent in the condo of Carol, Lee's friend for three weeks. When I got to Florida, I didn't feel too well. The flight had evidently raised my blood pressure, and so I asked to visit the hospital. It was found to be very high. I was in a panic for many days, doctoring, etc., for almost one whole week. I was in the pool every morning, exercising, and met nice ladies. One of them was a rabbi's wife. The second week, still in a panic with this blood pressure business, she told me her husband would be doing a service on Saturday morning. My blood pressure wasn't coming down. I found a doctor's wife in the pool. He would take my pressure every morning. I had never had this happen to me before. I was afraid I would die in Florida.

The night before I went to synagogue, I prayed all night on my knees, on my face, said the Rosary all night, and listened to a prayer tape that I had taken with me. I was scared. I did get some sleep, and when I woke up on that Saturday, I was the first one to enter the synagogue. I asked the lady at the door whether I should put a cover over my head. She directed me to this box, which carried dainty laced doilies. After covering my head, I went in and told the lady I was there to meet the rabbi's wife. The rabbi came out to meet me and directed me to where I would be sitting next to his wife, not him. He made that explicit. She had not arrived yet. She arrived at 10:15 a.m. Little did I know that on Saturday morning service, everyone just came in at whatever time they wanted to. I thought the service was at nine, and consequently, I was there before 9:00 a.m. That's how we Catholics do it anyway.

It was great. I kissed the scroll as they all did. I just followed the prayers in English as they did in Hebrew. They read backward, you know. The cantor I found, after service when he asked for visitors to make themselves known, was from a Rhode Island congregation, well-known to me, and had retired in Florida. He was very excited when I said I was not Jewish but "I was with God's people." I was accepted and asked to stay for lunch.

When I arrived home to Rita, she wondered where I had been for five hours. My spirit was highly lifted, and my day was complete. I thanked God for the experience and the healing that I ultimately expected.

We visited Florida two other winter trips staying at the Marriott (see epilogue The Pool of Miracles).

*   *   *

The Loss of My Son-in-law

I had a phone call. My daughter was asking me to meet her at the police station. I didn't know why I was going there, and when I got there, Caleb, my six-year-old grandson, greeted me with a policeman. Caleb had grease on his face, with his curious eyes telling me that he and Dad were driving when all of a sudden, the car was swirling around and they hit the D'Angelo's building. "Dad had a heart attack, and they weren't sure, but he might die. Mommy and the ambulance just left carrying Dad to the hospital." He died three days later (see epilogues The Truth about Love and Caleb).

My daughter made very rash decisions, eventually purchasing a house she couldn't afford in order to provide shelter for the rest of the adult children who are still hanging in. It is known that people in her situation make quick decisions without thinking things out. In her case, she was concerned for her children that had nowhere to go and were feeling the loss of their dad who had been a good dad and they were going to miss. They moved out of the rental that belonged to Rita, and I made all arrangements to have the house repaired and eventually sold it. God had a big hand in sending us a two-man team from Providence Rescue Mission who put the house in great shape during a spiritual experience (see epilogue Kingdom Builders).

After twelve years of caregiving to Rita, I found I was tiring easily on a 24-7 basis. There were pressures from my family; I was back in stressful life. Rita walked bent over, and after taking the bone-density test, we found that she had osteoporosis. Eventually, her hearing was being affected when we purchased hearing aids, which she seldom would wear. She had one eye operated on for cataract, which wasn't the answer to her sight problems. She never could see too well from the other eye, having had surgery at a very young age for lazy eye. At this point, I am over eighty. I was losing patience. I was suffering from anxiety. The safest thing for both of us was to separate. Faithfully, the Lord led me to Luke 6:38: "Give and it shall be given unto you; good measure, pressed down, and shaken together, and running over, shall men give into your bosom. For with the same measure that ye mete withal it shall be measured to you again."

We found a very warm environment for her in the now-called Pocasset Bay Manor, the independent living facility I had found for my aunt Angie several years ago. She is very happy there. She has a one-bedroom apartment, three meals a day, housekeeping, lots of card-playing, which she loves; and with my help, stopping in to assume the responsibilities that are lacking to fulfill her caring and personal needs, I spend lots of time with her during the week on catch-up and pick her up on Sunday morning for services at the church, keeping her with me all day. I, in turn, am blessed to be able to stay in her condo to care for her property until such time as there is a need for it to be sold. Prayerfully, never.

On The Set As An Extra

Gregory Peck—*Other People's Money*

He was so tired and needed the only one lady's/men's room for more than thirty people. I saw him walking up the path with his caregiver to my holding area when I was just about to use the facility. We were shooting in an old abandoned manufacturing plant in Connecticut.

I considered his age and status and waited. When he walked in the door, I invited him to use it first. His report as he came out was "Thank you, but we've got a real problem, it isn't flushing!"

I loved him. He was such a gentleman and great actor. That weekend of three days, where I made many new friends, and two nights shooting with a wonderful professional crew with consideration to the "extras" like me, I will never forget. Such fun!

Danny DeVito—*Other People's Money*

Ya gotta love 'im. Working with Danny on the set is a treat. His short legs take him here and there with ease, and such a professional! We shot outside scenes with him as extras. I was one of the stockholders.

I was the only one wearing a white fur hat and a short white fur jacket. We were getting ready to shoot a scene and were walking to our prospective areas when he stopped me and said,

"What are you doing here?" In my shocked state, I simply said, "The same thing you are doing here—shooting a movie." I was honored that he even noticed me, a mere "extra."

I was so impressed that I told everyone he spoke to me. One lady who had just arrived on the set that day answered with "He is a friend of mine, and he got me to come on the set today as an extra, and the reason he might have stopped you is that he has an aunt that looks just like you. He may have thought you were her." That explained it.

Steven Spielberg—*Amistad*

I was one of the five nuns. I never paid much attention to names and people except that I would respect them in their environment and honor their position. I didn't read much in my busy world, and I wasn't familiar with Mr. Spielberg, at least his face, at that time. I asked one of the nuns what he looked like. We were in a church and had just finished shooting that scene, and I figured he must be among the other men standing off in the distance. One of the nuns said, "There he is, standing over there, with the cap on."

At that time, I was working on *Rage of the Heart*'s world premiere and really wanted him to attend the opening if he was going to be in Rhode Island. The shoot was in Newport. Before I went to the shooting that day, I printed up this real beautiful invitation for him to attend. Now really!

Well, what did I have to lose? The timing seemed right, and I knew my position as "just" an extra, so I had to be coy, in the character of a nun, and would have to play the part.

I approached Mr. Spielberg. I was nervous, shaking, but he never knew. I was in my nun costume, and of course, we had no pockets. The invitation was tucked under my left armpit, and I had removed it in advance so that I would have it in my hand to get to the point, say my short speech, which I didn't have planned, and leave. The other four nuns tried to stop me before I left.

I approached him: "Mr. Spielberg, I'd like to present this invitation to you. It is a world premiere of a musical produced by a professional who was a priest. It opens on Thursday. Please accept it." He took it, opened it, and when he observed the date, he explained that he would not be in Rhode Island. He did, however, keep the invite. I made short of it and said, "I'm sorry you can't attend, but in the true sense of what a nun would do at this time, may the good Lord send you a special blessing" as I made the sign of the cross, turned on my heels, and gracefully left to join the others. When I got back, the girls were excited to hear how it went. It was fun!

Dane Cook—*My Best Friend's Girl*

I must admit that I felt somewhat grieved by the performance that he had to produce. I saw inside of him a young boy with a great deal of acting talent. As an instructor of film acting, he was, in my opinion, *doing* the role he was directed to do, the very best, with great reality. (see epilogue Never Say Never)

One instance in the movie, he had to take a sock in the face by his best friend. It was at the wedding when after the shoot, he dropped down in front of me with his hands over his face in shame. They called a "cut," and it was so real I could have cried. I leaned over, touched him on the shoulder, and said, "It's okay, grandma loves you."

He looked up, and I'll never forget the look in his eyes. One of the sixteen-year-old extra girls came over and asked if he would take a picture with her. I had my digital camera with me, and I used it. He was completely changed from the personality in the movie. A real nice guy!

There were many other movies as an extra in my time in Baltimore and even more as I returned home. All were special experiences, but these stand out as extra special.

The Future

Psalm 19:1-15 (The New American Bible—Catholic) talks about God's glory in the heavens and in the law. A psalm of David: God will protect me in my steps through the day because he promised me.

Psalm 46:10 (KJV) confirms, "Be still [quiet], and know that I am God. I will be exalted among the heathen, I will be exalted in the earth."

Psalm 119:111-112 (KJV) says, "Thy testimonies Have I taken as an heritage for ever: for they are the rejoicing of my heart. I have inclined mine heart to perform thy statutes always, even unto the end."

Quotes from Faithful Christians

> **Salvation**: "Our Salvation is good reason to rejoice. In prayer, let us remember all the joy we have drawn from the wells of Salvation. It should make quite a list." (William Stoddard, Hebrews 1:1-2:4)

> **Holy:** "Christ in us can manifest his holiness if we will yield our flesh to Him. Because of His everlasting love we know Him and He is faithful to mold us into His character of His Son Jesus Christ to make us Holy." (Patrick Morley, Hebrews 1:5-3:6)

> **Obedience:** "'How do we find God and grow in him? He said we must do what he says. Jesus had a theology of obedience.

The object of this obedience was a living person, not a historical norm, not a code of laws, but himself.' William Pannell has said, 'Just paint or get off the ladder.'" (Rebecca Pippert, Hebrews 3:7-4:13)

Priesthood: "We can be comfortable in the presence of a holy God. We can take our questions to Him to be sure we come in awe but the tremendous news is that we can approach the throne of Grace with confidence." (R. C. Sproul, Hebrews 4:14-6:18)

Promises: "Now you can relax for there is nothing to worry about. God cares and He keeps His promises." (Richard Lee, Hebrews: 6:9-7:10)

Please Him: "The misguided person who thinks all this is too difficult misses the point. The Christian life is far more than a fire escape from hell; it is a life of submission and obedience which result in joy and victory." (Bill Bright, Hebrews: 13:1-25)

Epilogues

FIDDLER ON THE ROOF

Each time the commercial comes up advertising that *Fiddler on the Roof* will be opening at Providence Performing Arts Center in Providence, it brings back all the wonderful performances I did in Baltimore, Maryland, during my twenty years in residence there.

My stage acting career afforded me to do this production with different groups in many different roles. I always considered myself to have some Jewish roots, but I couldn't find any. I am of Italian heritage. My Jewish friends, and I have made many, would comfort me by confirming that Italian mothers were just like Jewish mothers anyway.

I discovered Baltimore Actors Theater and began auditioning when I was cast as Sister Berthe in *Sound of Music*, my first musical. All the nuns were Jewish except myself. We were a repertory company, and my next role was Vera Charles in *Mame*. Coming from Rhode Island theater where I had performed mostly drama, I was ecstatic at having the opportunity to do musicals at last. I always held that dream in my heart since I loved singing and dancing. Other musicals followed until BAT was asked to cast *Fiddler* for a very exclusive Dinner Theater right smack in the middle of a Jewish neighborhood. I was cast as Golde and Yente and Grandma Tzeitle. There were three of us who traded roles and worked as stand-ins for each other. As Golde, in the dream sequence, I will never forget almost falling out of bed as Tevye wheeled the bed around and I was trying to get out of it. For anyone who knows it, that scene is supposed to be very scary, with lots of screaming from ghosts rising from the dead.

BAT did *Fiddler* several times. One performance was in one of Baltimore's Catholic schools. I'll not forget one evening returning from a rehearsal at the school, driving cautiously through a fierce snowstorm alone in my car. I slowed down and eventually stopped to witness seven beautiful reindeer gracefully prancing across Dulaney Valley Road about thirty feet in front of me. I played Yente in that production with a very talented Golde.

Soon, the local Jewish community center called me to play Golde for their performance. Each time, my feelings during the pogroms (persecutions to the Jews) that took place became very real to me. I lived through the performances with great emotion and many times broke down with uncontrollable tears and sadness. I remember my Tevye in this performance as having a very unusual sense of humor and was fun to work with. Two years later, I read that he committed suicide.

Sometime later, Towson University summer theater called me to play Golde. I would be working with a Yente that played Golde with me in the Catholic school performance. She was asked to do Golde but would be too tall as Tevye's wife. She brought my name to the director. She said, "I suggest her because she is the best Jewish mother in Baltimore." That sold him. We had become very close friends during that time because of our relationship in the last *Fiddler*. Actually, my stage career was very active, and most of my leading roles were Jewish mothers. When I found out who Tevye was, I was happy since I had worked with him in *The Man Who Came to Dinner* and he was a wonderful actor. *Fiddler* at Towson State was very successful and well-done in spite of Tevye's ensuing illness. It was filmed and played to full houses every night.

It wasn't too soon after the ending of that *Fiddler* when I had a call from the musical director from the JCC's performance that my Tevye was dying of AIDS. I knew of his history of dropping out of seminary for the priesthood and asked our friend if he would like me to pray with him. She emphatically answered, "Yes, I think he would like that." I did visit him. I prayed we would not be interrupted, and we weren't. He was very open, expressed his fear, but after our prayer together, he seemed calm. I felt in my heart he would meet his demise in peace.

My last performances of *Fiddler* were with BAT in their newly purchased Oregon Ridge Dinner Theater in Cockeysville, Maryland, with my first Tevye. I would soon be moving back to Rhode Island in the year 1987.

The feeling I got from the wonderful experiences I had while playing such colorful roles depresses me only to know that when I auditioned in New York for this exceptional musical for either role of Golde or Yente for a road company back about ten years ago, I was turned down. How could anyone who has played as many performances of this never-ending musical with memories of my Tevyes, daughters, their husbands, townspeople, rabbis, and my *Fiddler*s not be touched and become a wonderful part of their roots? Quite frankly, I found that I couldn't.

PS: I wrote the *Providence* journal this wonderful love story, and Connie Grosch picked it up and ran a video well edited by herself after two wonderful interviews in my home.

A FOND MEMORY

While rummaging through some old books today, something I hadn't done in years, actually, I came upon *The Book of Nature Myths* by Florence Holbrook, principal of Forestville School, Chicago (Houghton Mifflin Company, the Riverside Press Cambridge, Copyright 1902.) It was musty, but it really intrigued me. As I began to read the stories, I sneezed and snorted through the aged pages. It brought back memories of my favorite teacher, and when I went back to opening the cover, there it read, in faded ink, "To Edna from Miss O'Neill."

She was a nice teacher. She became friendly with Anna's and my mom. There is a long incident of how that all happened. Anna was my very closest friend since kindergarten where we started at Windmill Street School. She lived up the hill and on the other side of the school from my house. We grew to a very close, loving friendship. One day, a teacher came in and announced that Anna was skipping the second half of second grade into the third. In those days, school was planned in half terms. Anna began to cry and said she would not go because she didn't want to leave me. So guess what, they skipped me too. Well, the same thing happened in the fourth grade, and we both had to advance into Miss O'Neill's fifth-grade class.

Miss O'Neill, I assume, was in her forties, rather tall, was always crisply dressed, with very pretty blond hair worn short and close to her head. We all loved her. I remember she drove a small car to school every day. I can't be sure, but I think it was a 1936 Chevrolet. She surprised us one day, and she announced that she was taking Anna, two other students, and myself to the Gilbert Stuart Birthplace in Kingstown, Rhode Island. She had already consulted our parents. We were her very special students.

It was a very clear, beautiful Saturday to start off with, and the trip was fun. We packed a lunch and cooler and stopped on the road to enjoy bologna sandwiches, potato chips, and root beer. After visiting the house, which was very old yet to this day still survives, we headed for home. The sky was darkening, and we drove right into a heavy rainstorm. The road to the birthplace was narrow, with two lanes and ditches on either side in the year 1937. The weather wasn't easy to drive through, and I guess Miss O'Neill couldn't see too well, and we went off the road into a ditch. Naturally, the car tilted to one side, and we waited until the rain stopped before we got out. By this time, we were all crying, and as I look back, she had to feel some anxiety. But with confidence and comfort, she directed us into praying together that God would send us an angel.

Lo and behold, as we prayed, along came a car driven by a priest from nowhere in the gray day of dusk. Needless to say, he observed the whole picture and immediately set out to find help. This was in the days of no cell phones or communication from the car, but I am sure Miss O'Neill gave all information about us to the priest. When we arrived home after being rescued by firemen who had arrived to push us out of the ditch, our parents already knew that we were safe and on our way but would arrive later than planned. The day ended with thanks and praise.

The Book of Nature Myths consists of unusual short stories about animals with titles and interests, like one example, "The First Butterflies." It explains in great detail that they came from a beautiful thought of the Great Spirit.

I continued to sneeze through this book due to the mustiness so old but was happy to have found it to remind me of one of my fondest youthful memories of my fifth-grade teacher, Miss O'Neill, and my very best young friend, Anna—who now, at age eighty-one, is in a wheelchair after a stroke she had many years ago—and most of all, as a little girl, learning to trust the Lord in prayer.

ONE HUNDRED YEARS PASSED

I wasn't there, but I have heard about this lady born over one hundred years ago. They tell me she was born one and a half pounds, and in the days she was born, 1901, there were no incubators. She was kept in a warm oven—I have trouble believing this—but there is no longer anyone living to disprove it.

Her mother died when Amelia was four and a half years of age. Her father left to return to Italy, leaving two older brothers and a younger sister to be temporarily raised by relatives. He never returned before his death. It was customary for the man who had become widowed to return to his homeland to find another woman who would become his wife and mother for his children. Amelia lived in a warm family atmosphere. She was a healthy child and well cared for.

She married the brother of her cousin's husband. He would visit his brother quite frequently because he was very attracted to Amelia. He was a happy, joyful actor who had traveled the vaudeville circuit. She evidently liked his stories. He would share photos of his escapades onstage, which I am sure brought light to her life. His days on the road soon came to an end. He was needed in his father's store, where he became a skilled butcher.

They planned their marriage. Their wedding picture portrays a delicate lady wearing a lace headpiece over her close-cropped hair and a flowing floor-length veil. Her simple white portrait shows her neckline, ankle-length dress with accessories of a large beautiful bouquet of roses, and something that looks like a laced umbrella. Standing to her left is the handsome, clean-shaven groom wearing a high-collared white shirt with a white bow tie. His tuxedo label holds a rose, and he carries a pair of white gloves in his left hand.

She gave birth to a son. At the age of eighteen months, he developed a bad infection in the left hip that would produce thirteen years of operations and special care. Four years later, their daughter was born. Her husband became restless as a butcher, and soon after his father's passing, he built a neighborhood theater with an open roof where silent comedic and melodramatic films were shown. During the Depression, the neighborhood suffered poverty and the theater failed.

Both her mom and dad had to find work. He was hired as a butcher, and Amelia learned a trade working as a weaver in a mill. Mornings, each would go off to work very early in different directions. The older child was caring for his sister, both leaving for school. They never had an automobile, so her dad took a bus, as her mom found a driver who would pick her up. Her life became very busy with career, motherhood, and wifely duties. Summers added another responsibility. Her son would be confined to a body cast for three months in and out of hospital. Through their challenges, their strengths never wavered as two loving and devoted parents.

Years passed. Their son worked his way through college. He married, and he and his wife had a daughter. Four years later, carrying their second child, his wife was found to have lung cancer.

She died carrying the child at the age of thirty-three. Amelia was nurse to her daughter-in-law during this illness and continued to mother her four-year-old granddaughter until her son's marriage to his second wife nine years later.

Many changes were under way. Amelia and her husband were aging. The two found an appropriate apartment to live a more serene life. Her husband was soon to be found with cancer of the cranium. It was a long, agonizing illness until he died at the age of seventy-five. She turned all her possessions over to her children and made a final move to senior housing. Her next twenty-five years would be busy with new acquaintances. She lived a full life and always remained the focus of family gatherings, cooking all the aromatic Italian delicacies and traditional dishes.

In her early nineties, she had a fall and her health began to decline. By this time, her daughter had returned home, alone. She had divorced, and both children had married. Fortunately, the timing was right for her to assist with her brother to comfort their mother in her final years.

It's Monday. Visiting her today, I found two frail arms pushing the wheels of my mom's wheelchair, slowly inching herself from the dining room down to her bedroom at the nursing home. It's after lunch, and she'll soon be ready for her afternoon nap. The morning was spent on her art project in the activities room. It's hard keeping her spirits up now that she is tired and worn. She turned one hundred last July. She likes to sleep and shows signs of not hearing too well. Some days, she's somewhat alert. She'll sing by the piano while I play her familiar Italian songs. Her great-grandchildren, grandchildren, children, relatives, and friends will remember Amelia as a woman with dignity and style who always found a way to be available when needed.

As she opened her eyes from her nap yesterday, she said to my brother, "Take me home now, I just want to go home." She died peacefully, just short of 102, in a quiet, loving nursing home in 2003.

THE COMMUTER PLANE

The climate was darkening as we were waiting to board the US Air thirty-seat commuter plane headed for Palm Springs, California, leaving Phoenix, Arizona. Waiting to get into the plane, as the pilot passed me, I said, "Do we have to fly?" He answered yes. I came back with "Who is your copilot?" He replied, "God." Well, that was a comfort, but the black clouds continued to roll in upon us. A woman in a wheelchair boarded first. She sat in the front seat, right. I boarded next and was seated in the left seat, front, opposite her. We both sat directly behind the pilot. This was really too close for comfort. Marie, my traveling friend, boarded and found her seat in the back of the plane. I don't know how that happened; we bought our tickets together!

As this woman comfortably settled herself in her seat, we discussed the storm facing us. She was not comfortable with this flight because of the weather, so in conversation I tried to relieve her stress by telling her that the pilot told me God was his copilot. That didn't satisfy her as the plane began its ascent, however. I suggested we pray together. The plane continued on its course right into the storm. Up, up, and away! My right hand took her left, and we came in agreement to trust our Lord for a safe landing.

Suddenly, there was this pounding against the outside of the plane. I turned and asked the man in his single seat behind me, "What is that noise I am hearing outside the plane?" He explained we were in cold mountains and most likely we were in an ice storm. I turned my head forward to focus my eyes upon the panel in front of the pilot, which was quite colorful with flashes of red and green traveling side to side with unsteady markings. The pilot didn't seem nervous in any way until his windshield became covered with ice. There was no visibility. I must admit that this very new experience was beginning to upset me. Suddenly, my lady on my right said she was getting sick. I consoled her by finding a bag and passing it to her. The plane supplies for just this purpose were in a compartment on my side of the plane. "God is faithful. You'll be all right, I'm sure." At that point, the plane was swaying from side to side, jolting with funny movements. She was frantic. I immediately involved the gentleman behind me by asking him if he was a believer. He hesitated but finally, "Well, yes," so without further ado, I asked for his hand to pray in agreement that God keep us safe through this storm. He complied as we began to pray out loud and give thanks. It was very comforting to me to find a steady hand.

It wasn't long after that the plane leveled off. A bright light hit the windshield and melted the ice, showing a beautiful red sunlight. We had passed through the storm in prayer without realizing the time lapse. God had answered our prayer. The storm was over, but our destination was rerouted to Los Angeles. There was no way we could land in Palm Springs because of flooding beneath us.

With much delay, the plane finally landed in Los Angeles. There was a bus waiting to drive us to Palm Springs. The lady was assisted gently out of the plane, seated into her wheelchair, and was happy to be on the ground. Her son was to meet her in Palm Springs, and they were in contact by telephone shortly after landing. She said she would never fly again. Marie came down from the back of the plane and said with a chuckle and a smile, "Was that you praying out loud in the front of the plane?" "Yes, and I found a prayer partner too. You should know what was going on down there in the front of the plane." I told her of the miracle of the melt on the windshield. She made comment that at the rear of the plane, there was much conversation and concern with weather conditions and some anxiety too. Most had been through this before, evidently, since they travel this course frequently.

We boarded a bus that was waiting to transport us to Palm Springs. It was a long ride with heavy rains that made it longer. We arrived in our hotel around 1:00 a.m., tired and ready to just crawl under the covers and sleep.

We would spend two days in Palm Springs, taking bus tours throughout, passing the movie stars' homes, drinking date shakes—something new to these two northeastern broads—and, needless to say, enjoying every moment of it. This was the end of about seven days of what started out to be a learned elder hostel trip to Arizona, but because of weather conditions we encountered, with detours here and there, we learned that God had some real exciting new learning experiences we could write about. Our flight home was calm and relaxing.

THE MUSICAL IS BORN IN DIVINE PROVIDENCE

Frank was Enrico's brother. Frank was in one of my workshops, and his concept of me was that I was savvy about show business and would be some help to his brother. Enrico turned out to be a musical genius who had played organ at the cathedral at age thirteen, who eventually became a priest. A very well-known priest at that. During his years in Europe, his musical compositions became a great part of his life. The task at hand was that he was looking for someone to help him launch the world premiere of his *Rage of the Heart*, one of his compositions. He had left the priesthood.

Well, as God would have it, here I was in the middle of Enrico's dream. When I heard his music, I called upon Lou to help me get things going for the musical. I became Enrico's assistant producer in charge of casting. I summoned a dear lawyer friend of mine who ended up being executive producer because of his knowledge of theater law, had dreams of just something like this to get involved in, and took control of money, which no one else had. He was a longtime friend of mine from Actors Inc. and was a musician who played drums with my trombone brother. His wife was a professional actress, and a good one at that. I had worked under her in a production she directed in Bristol one summer.

A friend of Enrico's sent us a beautiful leading lady from Los Angeles; she loved the role, was from a wealthy family, and I went out to find her a house by searching the newspaper ads on a Sunday listing. She and her mom wanted a house on the east side, with stained glass windows, a piano, because she herself was a composer; and they would buy it or rent it for six months.

Believe it or not, we were a praying group in the cast, and God was at hand to see that this production went off. As it turned out, it did, but not without a hitch. There was lots of dissension because we were dealing with lots of artistic people who were definitely talented. We cast the show with a wonderful leading man and excellent supporting workers and actors. I ran an ad in the newspaper, called auditions, and a wonderful cast was gathered with two absolute leads fitting the roles perfectly. Preparation for this production took almost two years with lots of turmoil, but God was in control. The leading lady fell in love when she arrived in Rhode

Island. A young man had been cast first but did not add up to the role; however, they became very close, and he moved in with the family and supported her to the end. I had the opportunity to work with her and her family with comfortable quarters, which we found on that Sunday, perfectly fitting into a large home with all the specifications including the stained glass windows and the piano. They signed a rental contract for six months. The house was on the preferred list and was for sale.

Her dad bought her a brand-new, expensive car, which was stolen from the driveway of this east side home. It didn't throw them; the musical went off with rave reviews at the Veterans Memorial Auditorium. We who invested our $5,000 lost it to the cost of the production; some of the cast was disgruntled that they were not paid, but Katie from California and her family were happy to have had the experience. Katie married her Rhode Island love she found. They were both Christians, stayed in Rhode Island a couple of years working in a family church, but soon moved out west near her family at a church of their choice in musical ministry. The composer was very pleased. The executive director was happy to have finally been able to be part of this large undertaking, and Frank, Lou, and I happily sat back, proudly knowing that we got the show off the ground and into its position as world premiere. Believe it or not, it was a *miracle*!

THE POOL OF MIRACLES

Peggy rose from her chaise by the side of the pool with the determination to enter the pool and prove to the world around her that she could swim again. She wheeled over with her walker, supported by an elderly gentleman appearing to be her husband. Both seemed to be in their mid to late eighties.

Martha and I were in the pool; I was doing my leg exercises, walking back and forth while Martha, a somewhat avid swimmer, kept up with me in conversation. We actually struck up a comfortable friendship. The day before, I had noticed this very impressive woman sunning herself in a two-piece bathing suit in colors of brown and beige. Colors very conducive to her skin tones in good taste.

Peggy was very frail, about five feet in height, and as she struggled to descend into the pool, both Martha and I noticed that the gentleman seemed uneasy with the task to support her with her crippled legs that were very discolored in shades of red and black and blue marks. Martha made an advance out of the pool to assist Peggy in her determination, and I followed. Peggy struggled with the five steps, carefully holding on to the railing, descending into the area of three feet. She was definite in her requests and needs.

When she successfully joined us in the pool, I began to show her some of the aquatic exercises that I had learned to strengthen my legs in my recent bout with arthritis and sciatica. She followed each motion, allowing the buoyancy of the water to do its job. After five minutes of these simple exercises, she expressed a desire to swim. Martha and I glanced at each other but complied with her request. She shared with us that she had not been in the water for four years. Today was her day. Martha backed off about six or seven feet as Peggy left the wall of the pool where I stood and went underwater, swimming that distance to Martha. Martha assisted her ascent from the water since Peggy was unsteady but showed such pleasure. She requested that she do it again and swim back to me. For the second time, down she went, heading underwater. Successfully, her mission was accomplished. She showed such joy as she continued once more to swim back and forth. The three of us were overjoyed as her man friend watched with great excitement at the accomplishment of his determined woman. She was happy and tired with her accomplishment in her emersion of the pool, commenting to Martha and me, "You ladies have made my day."

In separate times together in conversation with Scott, her man, and Scott's daughter and her husband from Switzerland visiting her dad, Martha and I separately learned of their relationship. Peggy never knew Scott until she lost her husband. Scott, who was a very good friend to her husband, began to correspond with Peggy, who lived a long distance from Scott in Canada. Peggy suffered a very crippling automobile accident, losing her son. And Scott asked her to come live with him, and he would care for her. Scott confided that Peggy was a very good swimmer and diver as a young lady and was asked to swim in competition, but her father would not allow it. Peggy was able to show her desire with our assistance. The family surrounding her with all this love was very grateful for the assistance and love we showed. Peggy was ecstatic.

Martha and I assisted her the next day and the next. Scott finally took over, and when we left, they had one more week of vacation. They would be left alone since Scott's daughter and husband had to return to their home. Scott's grandson, however, had a business in Delray; and we all left confident that the two had someone near for their requirements. Scott is an alert ninety-two-year-old, and Peggy is a very self-sufficient eighty-six-year-old.

The pool last week served as therapy for a young crippled child. His mother and aunt and I became friendly in the pool as I learned that Timmy was in Delray for treatment. On the first day, his aunt walked around the pool, assisting Timmy in what I would call a support specially made for this exercise. His feet hung in the water through the two holes in the apparatus, which was round and held his body above the water. The attendant supported his head since his body was very limp and he had little control of his head and arms. The next day, his mother was in the pool. We conversed. The night before I learned their stay was ending, I had just finished my *Book of Miracles* by Pat Robertson. The next day at breakfast, I had planned to meet with them before they left. I gave them the book and shared my thought that they should keep it and refer to it often because I believed in a miracle for Timmy. They gratefully took it, knowing that he was a special blessing in their lives as were the two handicapped children they had left at home with their husbands.

Today, Peggy and Scott are sitting by the pool. It is cold, and Peggy has cream over her face with globs of it here and there. I smoothed it over her baby skin as she smiled with that very special smile and said, "Mommy's back."

Luck? The force or power which controls odds and which brings good or bad fortune. Our vacation ran around St. Patrick's Day. Coincidence? Two events happening at the same time by accident but appearing to have some connection. I don't think so.

My time around the pool during my Florida vacation in March 2006 added enriched depth and blessing to my life and to the lives of those who were touched by the miracle of divine providence. Miracle! That supernatural event or good happening regarded as an act of God.

THE TRUTH ABOUT LOVE

Love isn't just a word or a Valentine or a heart pierced with an arrow. It isn't something between two persons who see doves when they are apart with romantic thoughts of each other.

Love is *patient* like Chris when her husband suddenly suffered a massive heart attack one hot summer day while driving down Main Street in their town. The car stopped as it hit a building. Their six-year-old son was in the backseat, who thankfully was not injured. Her husband died three days later.

It happened at a time when her eighteen-year-old son was going through a very noxious time in his life, distracting everything in sight including himself. Love is *kind.* He was anything but kind to those around him. He was *jealous* of a girlfriend that which love is not. He was *arrogant* and all other ways love is not to be (1 Corinthians 13:4-8). It does not act *unbecomingly*; it does *not seek its own, is not provoked, does not take into account a wrong suffered, does not rejoice in unrighteousness, but rejoices with the truth, bears all things, believes all things, hopes all things, endures all things.*

Within these past seven months, Chris has been alone in what the world would see as a terrifying period of adjustment without her mate, with a daughter entering second year of college with no hope of financial assistance, an eighteen-year-old son behaving badly, a six-year-old son who was traumatized from the accident, and a busy twenty-one-year-old son struggling on his own, all missing their dad.

Chris began to *rejoice in the truth.* She began to *bear all things, hope all things, believe all things, and endure all things.* She had faith that if she behaved in the presence of scriptural love, the manifestation of her obedience would unfold in miraculous ways. In the portrayal of these facts of love, her nineteen-year-old daughter entered college with a grant, her six-year-old is recovering as he entered first grade of Catholic school, and her eighteen-year-old son went back to school and received his GED and is progressing and healing from past devastating days. Both he and his twenty-one-year-old brother are working closely with their six-year-old brother trying to fill their dad's place.

Love never fails, and neither does God's promises.

DEAR CALEB

One day, six years ago, I saw your daddy and mom who needed one of my stars in my heavenly kingdom to come to earth so I could give them help and comfort. Your daddy had a very heavy sick heart, and your mommy was very worried for your daddy. They came to me and prayed.

I looked through all my stars and chose the one I knew would bring new healing to daddy's sick heart. You were that star.

You went into this loving home of Daddy and Mommy, bringing with you all my gifts from heaven, and you did what I expected my special stars to do. You shared them with Mom, Dad, and your brothers and sister. You did exactly what I taught you in heaven. Your dad was able to feel the largest gift he could have been given in the earthly kingdom for the last six years of his life. You, my messenger.

Your daddy was one of those angel stars in my kingdom of heaven one day. I sent him to *his* mommy and daddy *fifty-four years ago.*

Now was time for him to return to my heavenly kingdom. He was driving his car when it happened, and as my heavenly angel, you were with him. You were there because of me, Caleb. You were carrying on what I had sent you to do. You were with your daddy right up to the time I called him.

Today your dad has become one of my stars again to be chosen out of my kingdom. When you grow up to be a loving father that I have chosen you to be in the earthly kingdom, I will send you one of my special stars, which will be your daddy.

Caleb, you will see him again, I promise.

In the meantime, continue to do my work as my special star. Spread my special gifts that are in you—love, joy, peace, patience, goodness, kindness, and self-control to your mom and family. Your mom knows best, and be good to her. I chose her and your dad as your parents. Be good to others, children, old people, and sick people; your daddy will be helping you from heaven. He was good on earth.

These gifts will never leave you, Caleb. I promise. You are now my son, and brother to Jesus, the next step on earth. Go to Jesus daily and ask for his help. The earthly kingdom needs my stars to keep shining.

You will help to make earth a better place to live. I sent you there for that. Your dad is safe with me.

Thank you, Caleb, for carrying the bright star into the home where your mommy will continue to do my work. Call upon me daily through my son, Jesus. He died on the cross for you. He planted his Holy Spirit in you to help you. His mother, Mary, loves you and will help your mother along with all of us in heaven to guide you and watch over all of you always.

Your loving father, God, and my son, Jesus.

Two days before the viewing of his dad's body at the funeral parlor, I prayed for the Lord to give a letter to Caleb so he would know why his dad was called home. I explained that I didn't want it to come from me. I was tired and was going to bed.

The next morning at 8:15 a.m., I jumped up out of bed, turned the computer on, and the Lord wrote this letter to Caleb, guiding my fingers to the right words. I had it laminated and brought it to the viewing. That night, Caleb had a very bad itch. Chris had him in a cool bath, yet Caleb was very uncomfortable and crying. I asked her to go to bed, and I would stay with Caleb until the itch subsided. It did after about one hour when he suddenly went into a deep sleep as I held my hands over him and called upon the angel Raphael, God, Jesus, and all the saints and angels available to heal him. He was healed. The next morning, he woke at 10:00 a.m. All had left for the church for the funeral. I asked Caleb if he wanted to have breakfast; he said no, dressed himself, and we got into a very hot car to head out to church. While cooling the car, I asked him if he wanted me to read the letter to him. He said yes, stuck his head through the two front seats, and I read it. "Did God really write that, Grandma?" I said, "Yes, Caleb. I was his vessel, and he let my fingers do all the work. This letter is yours to keep." He accepted it with some hesitation then said, "It's a little long though."

He faired the church beautifully, but when the bagpipers started playing, he completely broke down with heavy tears rolling down his cheeks.

KINGDOM BUILDERS

I had met Mark at a dinner for the Providence Rescue Mission one evening. He was introduced to the audience as one of the survivors of a drugged life and was now working at the mission to help others. He was working on hardwood flooring and was working at becoming proficient at it. He was an artist of a sort and enjoyed working with making things pretty. That night, I went up to him and met him, and he gave me a card with his name on it and asked me to call him if there was anything that he could do for me. I was thinking that he could be, in some way, instrumental in helping us with a relative of mine by finding work for him. This was at least three years ago.

Then shortly after my son-in-law's death, and my daughter was planning to move out, we would be needing a complete overhaul in the house, and we were thinking of replacing the floors with hardwood. I called him, and he said he would be right over. He was a delightful person to work with even with all the hurdles he had to jump over and roadblocks that made him stumble.

He called himself a kingdom builder. He told me he had a man that could help him rebuild the house and he was homeless and many nights slept in the mission. His name was Jack. Obviously, we were going on faith. I called upon the Lord and told him that we wanted to help these men out and give them some support in what they were planning to do. Jack knew his craft with hardwood floors, but it was my feeling that we didn't know how this would all end up. They started on the roof, which was leaking, and asked my grandson to help them one day to keep him busy. When I got there, the two workers had gone to Home Depot to pick up tools and supplies; and when they got back, my grandson had left after doing his job, which took ten minutes, picking up trash from the roof pieces that fell to the ground. Well, we were off to a good start. Trouble.

Never mind, don't bother with him. Just get this work done so we can put the house on the market. I asked, "Do you think that we could have Jack stay here?" Oh, Jack liked that, but we didn't have a bed. Remember, he was a one-nighter kind of guy at the mission. Jack went into the garage, and guess what he found waiting for him. A blow-up bed. Just like that. He blew it up, we got him blankets and a pillow, and there he stayed for the full duration of the work to be done. He did a good job. He took good care of the house. Mark was the runner; he was in and out, getting supplies for other jobs. New toilets, sinks, etc. Until one day, Mark got sick. He was out for about two days. Did very well, one of his friends fed him well, and he threw off a cold with no sweat. I was there every day.

All of a sudden, Jack was really ill. He was vomiting blood, so I decided it was time for me to start feeding him good food. God knows what he was eating, if anything. This whole thing was beginning to look like we should have gone another root. He said he went to the doctor and he had a bleeding ulcer. I looked up in my get-well books and found out that barley would be good for the stomach. I made barley juice and picked up some wheatgrass tablets for healing. Made soup and easy stuff to digest and nursed him back to good health. In the meantime, work was being done. Jack was a very good worker. He would work half the night, and we would pay them weekly for what they did. Mark got cleaning up the property with a couple of other men from the mission who needed work, so we were glad to be able to pay these men. Of course, they needed supervision, and as I write this, I feel the anxiety I felt then. But my cousin and I felt really good about putting these men to work. I didn't want to think that we were paying them for nothing. I had a good talk with Mark, and then they all buckled down and got the job done. Mark was a transformed Christian, and under the flooring, he kept printing scripture. The person living in that house now should be very blessed.

Mark and I were concerned with Jack's ailments, which kept popping up, but we'd come in agreement with prayer. Now that we were into the full swing, Lord, please see us through to getting this job done as soon as possible. Mark was very proud of his work. They laid hardwood flooring on the living and dining room floors, throughout the sunroom and the hallways on the bilevel home. They worked well together. Then Jack got sick again. I brought him to the hospital. Those were busy days for me. He was treated after I waited about two hours, and Mark was at the house getting things done. It was a full six-week project while I prayed daily with them and saw that the work was kept up with a goal that had to be met.

It ended up that God was our architect, Jesus was the builder, and the Holy Spirit was the beautifier. God's angels were right there working with Mark and Jack and the other random helpers that they brought in. It was costly; we did pay them well, especially Mark and Jack. But when it was all over, as much as we prayed with Jack for his salvation, we don't know what has happened to him. Mark said he was still visiting the mission from time to time. We had two angels helping a grandmother and her cousin get the house in shape to sell. And it sold without any questions. The buyers were a mother and her son with his daughter. They love it. We continue to keep in touch with Mark, but Jack needs prayer.

NEVER SAY NEVER

I found an ad in the newspaper for an instructor of modeling and acting, applied for it, and was hired on my experience and background in both areas. It was for the Warwick office of Casablancas Modeling & Career Center. I put my best foot forward, studied the curriculum, thoroughly followed the steps, purchased teaching books, put all my practical knowledge to work, and found, through my student evaluations and critiques, that I was a very qualified instructor. My many years as a stage actress, print and runway model were finally paying off.

One Saturday morning, I taught a class where one very astute student stopped me after class. She was star quality and recognized my spirituality. My childhood as a Catholic and deep searching into Christianity in Baltimore led me to my born-again experiences. My transformation was obvious to her as a nineteen-year-old in college. She asked me if I would accept a Sunday dinner invitation with her family. Of course, I accepted. She told me her dad was a pastor and they lived in Whitinsville, Massachusetts. The following Sunday, I was headed north, up Route 146, to find this modest home situated in a residential neighborhood on this cold month of November. Mom, dad, a pastor, and sixteen-year-old brother would be waiting.

We all enjoyed a simple Sunday afternoon, delicious food with good conversation. Her brother explained that he was a senior at Whitinsville Christian School and had accepted the position of running an assembly for the juniors and seniors and asked if I would be their guest speaker since I was an actress. Of course, I accepted. One month later, I made my appearance in this huge gym, with over one hundred students all sitting in the bleachers above my level. I was at a podium, looking upward, giving my talk on the gifts of the Holy Spirit, commitment, servanthood, and obedience to God. Young men and women, some with elbows on their knees on benches with no backs, sat wide-eyed and interested.

I ended with a question-and-answer session. One of the teachers asked what I would do if I was asked to do a role in a movie that was against my better judgment for a good sum of money. He asked, what if I had read the script in reference to the character, story, dialogue, etc., a sexual role for instance, and was offered attractive money, would I accept it? My answer was that I would "never" do anything against my Holy Spirit for money. I emphatically stated that I would "never" be associated with anything against the Lord's judgment of sin. That was on December 8, 1992.

During the years following, I was cast in several regional and national commercials; and by the year 2006, I would "never" do any more auditions for background roles in film. There were times incidentally when I needed money and accepted only background work in Rhode Island.

In August 2007, I received a call to audition for a movie. The role I would be auditioning for would involve only facial expressions that would start out as background but had the possibility to be upgraded during the shooting. This depended on whether the director and producer would approve on an upgrade. The female lead was a very well-known actress. The male lead I had never heard of. The bride's sister would be the female lead. I would be playing the grandmother of the bride that would make me also grandmother to the leading lady. I explained to the independent casting agency the decision I had made and would only audition if there were lines for this character role. I was told that I would be hired if chosen for my facial expressions in reaction to certain remarks thrown at me in one to three situations. I would also be raised from the floor about five and a half feet in a chair while the Jewish grandmother is danced around by the wedding guests, fall from the chair, but there would be a stunt double to take the fall. There would be a possibility for an upgrade with possible words depending on the decision of the director. This, of course, as a member of Screen Actors Guild, meant quite a bit more money than I would get as a background performer. I really didn't see anything wrong in just auditioning. I thought it had to have some good attached to it. Well, I went to the audition, and when I left, I was very unsteady about the role since the remarks I had to react to were pretty vulgar. I shared my feelings with the workers at the agency. When I arrived home, I prayed to God not to allow me to be cast unless He had some special plan for me in the final result.

The weeks passed, and I hadn't heard a word. I felt very comfortable about that. I hadn't passed the test, thank God, until one week, before the scheduled shooting of the grandmother's role, Hollywood, after viewing the video sent from Boston, informed the casting agency that they liked me for this unusual role. I would report the next day for a fitting at the costume office of the production company. The casting agent I auditioned for called me to tell me I had been cast in the movie as background, and another casting agency was handling the background actors and would be calling me regarding three days shooting in Boston at the Copley Hotel.

Since I was cast in background, this meant that I would need to travel back and forth between Boston and Cranston, working days from 7:30 a.m. to possible 10:00 p.m. Well, I knew at the age of eighty there was no way I would do that. Ha, there was my way out. I immediately called the assistant since I knew him quite well, having worked for him in other movies. I explained my dilemma. It was Labor Day, and we would be shooting the next day at 8:30 a.m. My requests were strong at this short time they had given me. The production company of the movie would have to see to it that all expenses would be paid. All this was being discussed while I was supposed to be enjoying our annual family picnic in Bonnet Shores. The phone calls were going back and forth with my instructions and requirements for a hotel that night and all other nights until the end of my sequences in the movie. He was having trouble trying to contact more than two hundred extras for the shoot, but I really wasn't concerned at this late date with his challenges. If they wanted me, they would have to make the proper arrangements for my concerns, my accommodations. I emphatically said I would not show up unless these were met. At this point, I was very upset about having to accept this role in the first place. I did everything to discourage them from using me. I was working every inch of pressure on them, hoping they would let me go from the commitment and find themselves another grandmother. I called some very influential agent friends of mine in New York to find out what I should do in this case. I wanted out. Would I get blackballed from the union? I felt that I was getting the squeeze. The advice I got from my friends didn't really help my situation. I went to God and put it in His hands. His final act came through with approval, and my orders were met. I left our family picnic early in order that I pack and get the train and check in to the Hilton Hotel, Back Bay, for a good night's sleep.

The next day, after a full day's shoot, time with the hairdresser, makeup artist, and being told I had a stunt double for the "fall," I was escorted back into waiting with 250 extras for my important role as the star's grandmother. I seemed to be signaled out as a special person with a principal role in this movie yet not being recognized or paid adequately. Nevertheless, I stayed my ground as an extra, made wonderful friends, and was able to find prayer partners for the vulgarity being used in the movie—my confrontations with the leading man and having to swallow his gross actions. At one point, I retaliated with slapping him in the face with a pork chop at the wedding hors d'oeuvre table. That shot ended up on the cutting room floor. He complimented me afterward on my acting talents, as did the producer and director who came over to me, saying I was doing a phenomenal job. I really didn't care about their opinion. It was very hard for me to even be there. But my fight was strong, and I felt something stronger inside me pursuing.

The wrap was called at 10:00 p.m. No reservation had been made for me to stay for that night, so I had to call production to get me a room at the Hilton. They were met, and I stayed at the Hotel Hilton, Airport for that night. I was blessed to have had a very dear praying Christian working with me as an extra, and I invited her to spend the night in my room. She would have had to travel back and forth to her home because of the next day's shoot for 8:00 a.m. After a good night's sleep, the next morning I called production for transportation to Back Bay, where we were shooting at 8:00 a.m. The next day was a longer day. We were cramming to get everything done. The stunt double showed up; and after my ten times shooting the scene of falling off the chair from five and a half feet off the floor the day before, she took a thumping fall, which filled in my shots, and she was done. I have to admit, the three people left holding me during my falls the day before made sure I did not hurt myself.

That night, after shooting all day, again arrangements hadn't been made for me to stay over for the next day's shoot. In fact, one of the director's assistants came over to me and let me know that I was demanding too much from them. This was at 11:00 p.m. I called the production office and spoke to the assistant in charge of my demands, and she was appalled that the set workers and DAs were treating an eighty-year-old with such disrespect. She explained her mother was eighty and she would certainly see that I would be taken care of. She made arrangements for that night's lodging at the Hilton, Airport again. The next night, the same thing happened at 10:00 p.m. The next thing I knew was that she was in charge of my wants and needs and she took complete control. Thank God for cell phones; on the last evening of the shoot, she called me back in time before I was about to get into a car with a very young sweet lady who would be driving back to Rhode Island. She recognized me as the grandmother and was kind enough to befriend me during the shoot. She had also offered a ride to another person that really did not appeal to my inner spirit, and my prayers were answered. Production called at that very moment and stopped me from getting into the car. She had made the reservation. The van had been in a traffic jam in Boston that would delay my pickup, so she sent two guards to stay with me outside the Copley, where we had "wrapped" our final shoot. I soon was picked up safely and transported to my destination for one more night's lodging.

The next day I was through. I was driven to the train station, took the fast train home, and was happy to have once again lived through another rough assignment in my exciting life. I must admit, God does give me some tough challenges; and in this case, I had just completed acting in a movie I said I would "never" be affiliated with. I obediently followed through to the end, only trusting God for every move. I was a witness to many people who knew of my dilemma.

When I called the union on my arrival home, I explained the fall and other requirements for upgrade, and they proposed them to production, who acted upon them immediately. This unrated movie upgraded me with special credit as the grandmother. When we are working for God and are in His plan, we are well protected. It is His call.

THE KINGDOM AWARD

What is this stage and set produced, and who directed it?
Who wrote the actions that we take, to cross down stage or sit?
To play the rolls the author calls, a villain or a king?
To hide behind a mask so cold, a puppet on a string?
To serve Director at his call, be recognized and praised?
When critics say "a job well done", after the curtain's raised?

It is a human dynamo, who knows his subject grand,
Directs the actors one on one, receives it on demand.
Obedient we are to world, where Satan calls the shots,
His lies attract the human mind, our stomachs tie in knots.

But then the Revelation comes, the greatest drama played.
The Hero is the Lord himself, our lives are greatly weighed.
The seven churches are ourselves, the characters unloosed
By seals of Chapters six and seven, four horsemen introduced.
The trumpets sound and sevens are gone, the antichrist the lead,
he stalks across the gallant stage, but Christ comes to impede.

Majestic as He takes the stage, the enemy retreats.
He carries all His hosts with Him, His gallantry repeats.
The drama now in one accord, the enemy now falls,
There are no critics to be seen, the King directs us all.